# Unbelievable Crimes Volume One

## Unbelievable Crimes, Volume 1

Daniela Airlie

Published by Daniela Airlie, 2023.

UNBELIEVABLE CRIMES VOLUME ONE

**First edition. January 13, 2023.**

Written by Daniela Airlie.

# Table of Contents

Unbelievable Crimes Volume One..................................................1

Prologue .............................................................................3

A Mother's Worst Nightmare .......................................5

The Girls Under The House .......................................13

An Extreme Obsession..............................................23

A Familiar Face.......................................................29

If You Loved Me, You'd Do This For Me .................37

You'll Find My Footprint On My Dad......................45

Love Is Blind .........................................................53

Terror At Tiede Cabin ............................................61

The Tucson Pied Piper ...........................................69

Like A Woman Scorned ..........................................77

A Most Sadistic Gang..............................................85

Mother Or Murderer? ............................................95

Final Thoughts.......................................................103

# Prologue

The horrors that one human can inflict on another human is something that intrigues all of us true crime followers.

We read about crimes and watch documentaries that expose the horrific acts of brutality and depravity that people carry out on one another. It's a morbid fascination, something we are drawn into learning about even if it makes us feel nauseous or uncomfortable. We don't get drawn in for the same reasons we watch, say, horror movies or soap operas, for example. We are interested in true crime because the events truly happened. Often, horror movies are too far-fetched to be true. But *true* crime is just that - it's real. And perpetrators of crimes, murders, and acts of depravity are just like us.

Of course, murderers and serious criminals may be wired differently, but the scary thing is, we can rarely tell. They can blend in with the rest of us, and they're not always the introverted, isolated psychopaths the media often portrays them as. Murderers can be charismatic, likable, and downright believable. This is why I feel true crime is such an intriguing topic for us. It exposes the capability of human depravity, and it shines a light on the fact that it can happen to anyone - and it can also *be anyone* who carries it out.

We all know about the over hashed tale of Ted Bundy or the vile acts Jeffery Dahmer committed. There have been so many books and TV shows dedicated to these crimes it's hard not to know about them. Some cases seem to have longevity and have documentary after documentary dedicated to retelling the story. While these crimes were undoubtedly horrifying, and I truly believe we should never forget the victims or their suffering, I would like to cast the spotlight on less-covered crimes that were just as abhorrent.

3

Before we begin, I'd like to offer a quick word of caution about some of the cases covered in this book. True crime is, by nature, an emotion-evoking topic, but some crimes are particularly brutal to hear about, including ones involving sexual assault, domestic abuse, or crimes involving children. This book touches on cases that involve these themes. With that said, let's begin.

# A Mother's Worst Nightmare

Child killers are such a horrifying category of crime cases that there are a number of TV shows and documentaries dedicated to the topic. To imagine a child or a teenager feeling the urge to end another human's life is almost beyond comprehension, but sadly, child homicide is a very real occurrence in true crime. We digest these tales with bated breath, hoping there's an explanation behind a minor committing such atrocities as rape, extreme violence, and torture. Sometimes, it's revealed the child was reenacting the violence and abuse they suffered at the hands of adults. Other times, brutal movies (not made for young eyes) have been blamed for a child carrying out horrific killings.

In the case I'm about to cover, I'll confront the idea that a child carried out a murder for no other reason than for their own pleasure. To label a child as evil, to some at least, may be unthinkable, but let me tell you about the story of Paris Bennett and see how you would describe the motive behind the cruel murder of his 4-year-old sister.

Paris' mother, Charity Lee, felt her world crash around her on February 5, 2007, when the police arrived at her workplace, Buffalo Wild Wings, on the outskirts of Abilene, Texas. The single parent of two hadn't had the easiest of times bringing up her children, but she did the best she could. Despite being born into a relatively wealthy family, Charity had been through her fair share of turmoil in her life.

When she was young, her father died, and her mother was accused of the murder, although she was later acquitted. With her father gone, Charity was left with a mother who didn't offer her much in the way of love or affection. Like a lot of children do, Charity tried to do whatever she could to please her cold parent, but nothing seemed to work. By the time she was 17, the teen was suffering from heroin addiction and a plethora of mental health struggles, and her mother had kicked her out of the family home.

Charity found herself living in a halfway house, where she managed to break away from the dark path she was heading down and got control of the hold heroin had over her. She was still suffering from depression, but in early 1993, she received some news that would help her overcome her battle with mental health problems: she was pregnant with her first child.

In late 1993, her baby boy was born. Charity named him Paris, and it was love instantly. Paris' dad left the picture shortly after, leaving the boy's upbringing solely up to Charity, who thrived at motherhood. Paris grew up to be a happy, funny, incredibly creative, and inquisitive child who excelled at drawing and creating things. He was also a certified genius with an IQ of 141.

In 2001, Charity found out she was expecting child number two with a new partner, and she was over the moon. The same can't be said for Paris, however. He refused to acknowledge the imminent arrival of his sibling, much less show any excitement or curiosity towards the new family member. In fact, even just mentioning the baby would upset eight-year-old Paris.

When Ella was born in the spring of 2002, Paris' once hostile feelings toward his sister seemingly evaporated. The once jealous, angry child displayed acts of love and adoration towards his baby sister, which was bound to have been a relief for Charity, who expected Paris' coldness towards Ella to continue after her birth. It seemed as soon as he saw his tiny sister, Paris stepped up and became the perfect big brother: loving, protective, and willing to help take care of the newborn. This would have been a big help to Charity, who was again a single mother since her relationship with Ella's dad had fizzled out.

By 2005, Charity moved her little family back to Texas to take care of her mother, who was battling cancer. After being clean for over a decade, the pressures of being a single parent and trying to get her promotions business up and running had taken their toll, and Charity found herself seeking out drugs. She went on a cocaine bender for six months, something 11-year-old Paris bore witness to. In a bid to get back on track, Charity took the family to Alabama to live with Ella's dad, a move that didn't last long. The kids were uprooted back to Texas to live with their grandmother. Charity and her mother still had a strained relationship, and drugs were still a constant in the mother-of-two's life despite her attempts at getting clean.

Charity would later say that she felt this moment in Paris' life was pivotal for him since she'd let him down and disappointed him. Perhaps she felt that this was why Paris began acting out, with one episode being especially concerning. While playing on their grandmother's ranch, Ella and her friend were upset when Paris broke one of the toys they were playing with. Charity noticed her baby girl was crying, and after figuring out Paris had caused Ella's distress, she reprimanded the young boy. This seemed to trigger something in Paris.

Instead of staying in time out like his mother told him to, Paris headed to the kitchen, grabbed a large knife, and raced away from the ranch in a highly emotional state. A member of staff who worked at the ranch noticed Paris running with the knife and informed his mother and grandmother, both of whom immediately set out looking for him. After a panicked search, Paris was eventually found, but he was inconsolable. He waved the knife at anyone who tried to touch him, and it was a perfectly timed lunge from his grandmother who saw the blade taken from him. When the weapon was removed, Charity hugged her distressed boy, and he collapsed in her arms, both of them ending up on the floor.

Paris was taken to a psychiatric hospital where he stayed for a week, but unsatisfied with his treatment there, Charity brought him back home. It would take well over a year for the psychiatric facility to properly update Paris' record, by which point he'd already committed the murder of his little sister. His notes explained how he was "obsessed about shooting and killing," and one can only contemplate if Ella's fate would have been different if these records were seen before his cruel murder of his younger sister.

After the worrying episode at the ranch, Charity decided a fresh start was needed for the family, so she moved to Abilene, Texas. Charity began work at Buffalo Wild Wings to support her children, although it wasn't uncommon for the mother to be home late due to the shift pattern. This meant she'd often need to enlist the help of a babysitter, and she found one she felt was a good fit. Paris liked her, and she was good with Ella. She had no qualms about leaving her babies with the babysitter, but she didn't bank on Paris being able to manipulate their sitter into leaving her shift early. But that's just what happened, and this begins the tragic tale of Ella's death. On February 5, 2007, police walked into Buffalo Wild Wings and told Charity there was an issue at home. When the worried mother asked police to take her to be with Ella, they had to inform her that they couldn't: she was dead.

Barely able to take in what she'd just been told, in a daze, Charity then asked to be taken to Paris. She was then told she couldn't see her son because he was in custody, suspected of killing little Ella.

Rewind back to 10 pm on February 4. With Charity waiting tables on a busy Sunday, Paris set about convincing the babysitter she could go home early. He'd spent the hours before looking up adult sites on the internet, browsing violent content that he'd found by using phrases like "sadism" and "S&M." With the babysitter eventually gone, Ella was left with her older brother.

He would go on to violate her, getting more and more violent with her as he sexually assaulted her. He would end up using a knife, stabbing the helpless four-year-old 17 times. He didn't do it quickly, either; the boy enjoyed watching the girl in pain and would slowly stab her and pull the knife out. He would beat and choke his helpless victim. The wicked boy got more excited as his torture went on, eventually killing the girl. He left his semen at the scene of the crime, Ella's bed, as well as the lifeless body of his sister. He never tried to cover up his crime; in fact, he was so unbothered by what he'd done that he managed to fit in a phone call with a friend after the atrocities he'd just carried out. It was only after this that he decided he should call 911, and although he admitted to killing Ella, he said it was an accident.

"I woke up, and I was hallucinating," Paris told the operator, who asked him to perform CPR on the girl. Paris was hesitant, telling the call handler that it wouldn't help because she'd already died. The operator eventually got Paris to try to revive his sister, talking him through carrying out CPR while an ambulance was on its way. As soon as authorities arrived, it was plain to see that Paris had never attempted any kind of resuscitation despite acting like he was following the operator's instructions. Paris was audibly crying, yet no tears fell from his eyes.

Police took Paris in for questioning, and his story was unconvincing. He told officers that he'd been hallucinating that his sister was a demon whose head was alight, like a pumpkin on fire. He said the demon - his sister - was goading him, laughing at him, so he took action by stabbing her to death. It didn't take long for this tall tale to be rebuked. Ella's autopsy proved she'd been sexually assaulted and tortured prior to her death. A search of the family computer also exposed Paris' internet search history, which also included snuff films. Any denial on Charity's part about her son being guilty of this terrible crime had all but disappeared. She now had to face the sickening truth that her little boy had carried out this unthinkable crime. Charity confronted an incarcerated Paris, and his reaction was one of anger. When his mother confronted him about the semen at the crime scene, Paris stormed away and punched a wall.

There was no way he was getting away with it, so Paris had no choice but to confess to the murder of Ella. He told police he'd planned the death of his sister in order to cause his mother immeasurable amounts of pain. He admitted that his plan at one point was to kill Charity too, but decided that living without her children would be far more painful for her.

Paris was held in a juvenile facility, although his antisocial behavior didn't seem to dampen. He would attack other juveniles for no apparent reason. He flooded his room, attacking the staff that tried to intervene. He would say disturbing things about younger individuals in the youth lockup. He had to be reprimanded by staff for the way he spoke about his younger peers at the facility. Paris was evaluated while detained, and one psychologist wrote that Paris was "smiling" when discussing the murder of his baby sister. Other members of staff also reported that the manipulative teen had tried to coax his mother's new address out of them. Charity was, understandably, unable to stay at the Abilene property where Ella was killed, so she moved to San Antonio, although she didn't want Paris to know her exact whereabouts.

Paris was given 40 years in jail for killing Ella, and to many people's surprise, Charity visited her son regularly. Paris would often be cruel to his mother on these visits, telling her he enjoys watching her pain and even physically attacking her in one instance. He pinned her to a wall by her throat, stopping her from breathing. Still, perhaps giving new meaning to the term "unconditional love," Charity continues to visit Paris.

Paris has essentially grown up at the Ferguson Unit Texas State Prison and has spoken out for several interviews since his incarceration. He fully accepts what he did, insisting that he suffers no mental illness and isn't insane. Charity feels differently. She says she knows her son is a psychopath, she understands he may still harbor a desire to kill her, and she admits there's nothing she can do to help him. Still, she won't give up on him, she says.

Charity went on to have her third child in 2012, a boy she called Phoenix. She allows Phoenix to speak to Paris on the phone occasionally, a move she admits she's been heavily criticized for. She explains this decision is to teach her young son how forgiveness looks. Of course, Charity still has Ella at the forefront of her mind. Ella's last painting at school was of butterflies, something Charity now associates with her little girl.

Paris Bennett will be eligible for parole in 2027. If you watch interviews with him, it's hard not to think that he's capable of repeating the same sadism and violence he carried out in 2007. Even as an adult, there's a cold, menacing demeanor to him. He speaks clearly and calmly but without emotion or feeling, evoking an uneasiness for the viewer. If Paris is granted freedom, there's a very real risk that he will offend again, and Charity would likely be who he sets his sights on.

# The Girls Under The House

There are a few notable "women in the basement" cases, whereby a male captor kidnaps their victim or victims and keeps them in his basement, often to be sexually abused. Josef Fritzl is the first one that comes to mind, although he didn't imprison a stranger; it was his daughter, Elisabeth. He kept her beneath the family home, which he shared with his wife and children, and impregnated her multiple times, three of which resulted in Elisabeth giving birth. There was also the case of Natascha Kampusch, who was just ten years old when she was taken in broad daylight and kept in a cellar until she was eighteen when she managed to escape.

Cases like these often include themes of rape, violence, and power over the captive. The case I'm about to cover is no different, other than in two aspects. Firstly, it didn't become worldwide front-page news as the others did. And secondly, unlike most abduction cases, this kidnapper would utilize a "catch-and-release" strategy, where he'd let his victims go after he was done with them. Sometimes, he'd keep them for months, sometimes years. Either way, they'd all endure the same violence, sexual abuse, and terrifying isolation as each other.

John Jamelske was born in DeWitt, New York, in May 1935. He grew up an above-average achiever, and after working as a manual laborer for some years, he eventually amassed enough of a savings pot to invest in property in California. He would live a financially comfortable life alongside his wife, Dorothy, whom he married in 1959. The couple had three children together, but as the years passed, Dorothy's health deteriorated. Cancer caused her to become entirely bedbound by the late 80s, around the same time her husband would kidnap his first victim. John Jamelske would cite his wife's poor health as the catalyst for his desire to kidnap and rape women. His wife was no longer able to sleep with him, so John decided the next best option would be to abduct women off the streets and keep them in his specially-built bunker under the house. Here, he'd be able to have his way with them whenever he chose.

His first victim was a child. He lured the 14-year-old into his car under the guise of giving her a ride to her friend's house. Instead, he took her to his mother's property, where he chained the young girl up. The captive didn't recall too much about the car ride but sobered up quickly when she woke up in a dark, damp, and cold room with a chain around her ankle. The girl didn't realize it right away, but she wasn't in a dank room at all. She was in John's mother's well, just outside her home, but that setup wasn't going to work for long. Eventually, John moved her to his house and placed her in what would be christened *The Dungeon*.

The steel door entrance to The Dungeon was hidden behind a storage shelf, which John would drag out of the way before marching the young girl inside. You could only access The Dungeon by crawling on your hands and knees in a narrow tunnel that led to yet another steel door. Through here, you had to climb down a small ladder where you ended up at the heart of The Dungeon. John tied his captive's shackled ankle to this ladder and let her know, in no uncertain terms, why she was there.

For over two years, the teenager was subjected to daily rapes, emotional and physical abuse, and threats towards her family should she ever expose John or his dungeon. Hygiene was something that John had thought of, albeit poorly. The teenager (and the victims that would come after her) was forced to use an old bathtub and garden hose that only ran cold water to clean herself. When the tub drained, the dirty water flooded The Dungeon floor, causing the restrained captive to essentially stew in the damp, chilly puddles until they vaporized.

The toilet situation was just as dire. Perhaps John made it purposefully degrading by placing a seatless chair frame over a bucket to create a makeshift loo. As ugly as it was impractical, the victims had no choice but to use it. Over time, John decided The Dungeon needed some decoration, so the walls were scrawled with phrases such as, "Peace to all who enter here" and "Bring on the pain." The word "hate" was carved in red writing on the wall, as well as "Ready to ruckus." He also hung a crucifix at the entrance of The Dungeon.

The young girl's family were distraught at the teenager suddenly disappearing, and with no leads as to her whereabouts, they feared the worst. While John didn't know just how little the police knew, he figured they'd be looking for the girl. To help pacify the worried family, he forced the teen to write letters to them and leave them voicemails saying she was okay and she'd come home soon. John had photos of the girl's family and threatened to harm them if she ever went to the police.

After a little over two years, John decided it was time to let the girl, now aged 17, return home. She told her family what John had told her to: that she simply ran away. She was too afraid to tell the truth for fear of her family being murdered.

A few years passed before John would acquire another girl to keep in The Dungeon. He would go "cruisin'", as he put it, for potential victims. Around 1995, he found his second one, another 14-year-old. He lured her into his car by pretending he needed help to deliver a package. Again, the girl awoke in a strange, cold place. She was in The Dungeon.

She put up a fight; there was no doubt about it. She lashed out as hard as she could, but she was shackled to the ladder, just like the girl before her. And, just like the first victim, she was subjected to daily rapes, threats, and abuse. She was forced to keep a diary, too, of the things she did throughout the day. The diary-keeping routine was something John would go on to make all of his victims keep. Letters symbolized certain actions. For example, "B" suggested the girl bathed that day, and "T" meant they brushed their teeth. "R" meant they'd been raped. To me, the fact that John encouraged the girls to use the word "rape" here when describing what he did to them lets me know he was fully aware what he was doing was wrong, yet he would later say he thought the girls were complicit in these assaults and that what he did wasn't that bad.

John would also record the abuse on a video camera. He told his victims that this tape was for his "bosses," and to ensure compliance from the girls, he told them the less they resisted during these recorded rapes, the quicker his bosses would authorize their release. One of his victims made a plea directly to the camera, telling the faceless "boss" that it'd be better if he let her go home. Little did she know, the only person who'd be watching that tape would be the person filming it.

Again, when he was done with victim number two, he set her free. Unlike the first girl, she told her mother everything. It's speculated they never went to the police for fear of John following through with his threat to slay the girl's family if she told anyone what happened.

When it came to victim number three, John ramped up his sadistic abuse.

Around 1997, he chose an adult to abduct: a 53-year-old Vietnamese woman. She was again lured into John's battered 1975 Mercury, this time under the ruse of him needing friends. Before she entered the vehicle, they exchanged pleasantries as best they could, with the victim not speaking much English and John unable to understand Vietnamese. The woman and her soon-to-be kidnapper drove around the streets for hours, talking as best they could. Eventually, John brought her back to his house and threw her in The Dungeon, securing her to the ladder before locking the door behind him.

A few days later, the woman's boyfriend contacted Syracuse police to report his partner missing. Again, there were no witnesses, no leads, nothing for the police to investigate. Nobody was coming for the woman tied up in John Jamelske's cellar, where she was raped on a daily basis and forced to do household tasks for her captor. He was especially violent with this victim, too, hitting her with such force he damaged her ear. He was also emotionally abusive towards his victim and once put a life-sized skeleton next to her while she slept. He took great joy in the fear his victim expressed when she awoke and believed she was lying next to human remains.

After John was done with the woman, he dropped her off at a bus station with a little money. She headed straight to the police station and told them everything she'd been through the past few months: rapes, beatings, being shackled in a cellar, and the cruel tauntings at the hands of her captor. She had a description of the man who did this, too. He was around 5' 8", had a birthmark on his head, was overweight, and she guessed he was in his mid-40s. None of this mattered; the police were hesitant to take the woman's story seriously. She later said how detectives pounded the table with their fists when she was telling them about her ordeal, shouting at her that she was lying. The inaction of law enforcement meant John Jamelske was free to "go cruisin'," as he put it, and seek out a new victim for The Dungeon. With his wife passing away in 1999, he was even more inclined to drive the streets for new prey, and in May 2001, he'd strike again.

He rolled his beat-up sedan beside a young woman walking to her friend's house. She had just got off work and took a shortcut through a bad neighborhood where a group had been following her and intimidating her. It was dark, and the woman was understandably frightened, speeding up her pace to get to the safety of a busier street. John wound his window down and offered the woman a lift to where she was walking, which the woman accepted gratefully to escape from the gang tailing her. The car journey was hazy for the woman. She'd been drinking with friends for a short while after finishing work at Outback Steakhouse, but she was alert enough to become worried when the man taking her to safety was heading in an unknown direction. She even tried opening the door of the speeding car without any luck. Eventually, she wound up where all John's victims did: The Dungeon.

I can't think of anything more sobering than waking up naked in a freezing, dark cellar, chained up and unable to see anything around you. For terrified victim number four, that's exactly what happened, and for the next two months, her life would revolve around keeping her captor happy in order to survive. Her disappearance was reported to police, and helicopters were deployed to search the areas where the woman was last seen, but yet again, the investigation yielded no leads.

The victim was told there was no one coming to save her because the police were involved in her capture. John even contemplated out loud about selling her on the internet for tens of thousands of dollars. These were lies told to help him dominate and control his victim, to make sure she felt the idea of escaping was hopeless. To comply is to survive, and that's what the woman did. Of course, she'd have fleeting thoughts about somehow knocking her abuser out cold and making a break for it. However, the conniving kidnapper had already thought about this scenario and made sure to lock The Dungeon door behind him every time he entered. Should any of his victims try to harm him and escape, they'd need to figure out the combination lock number first.

Two months later, John entered his dungeon of iniquity and threw the victim's clothes at her. "You're going home," he told her matter-of-factly. Who could blame the woman for thinking this was just another of John's mind games? She got dressed as instructed before a hood was pulled over her head and her hands were bound by handcuffs. She truly believed she was about to be killed, so when she was dropped off right outside her mother's home, she was as confused as she was elated. One thing bothered her, though: she'd never told her abuser anything about her mother, let alone where she lived. Still, she raced into the house, and the police were immediately called.

She gave authorities all the information she had, including a thorough description of the cellar she was held in. She memorized the graffiti on the walls as well as the peace sign and crucifix that was ironically hung up. The only thing she couldn't tell the police was where this place was. She drove around with a detective to see if she could pinpoint the house, but she was unable to make a positive identification, which is understandable since she only got a very brief glimpse of John's house prior to being locked in his cellar.

The case went cold quickly.

After getting away with these abhorrent crimes for so many years, John was incredibly confident in his ability to evade the police. He felt untouchable and would become more than brazen with his next young victim. The 16-year-old, a runaway whom John would force to take sedatives in order to carry out his wicked and depraved acts upon, was treated somewhat differently from the victims who came before her. While she endured daily sexual assaults, traumatic mind games, and John's brainwashing tactics, she was allowed upstairs, unlike his other captives. The doors and windows were securely locked, so escape was almost impossible, however. Soon, the shameless criminal was taking his young victim out of the house with him, too. His brazenness turned out to be the end of John Jamelske's reign of terror over the women walking the Syracuse streets alone.

He brought his teenage captive with him on errands and even took her bowling on at least one occasion. In the spring of 2003, he took the girl to a karaoke bar with him. Patrons noticed the pair looked like an odd couple; he was an older man who resembled the colonel from a famous Kentucky fried chicken franchise, with his thick glasses and gray goatee. She was a young African-American woman who looked desperately overwhelmed and out of place. Still, nobody approached the duo, and John was getting increasingly unabashed about where he brought his victim.

A few days after visiting the karaoke bar, he took the girl bottle collecting. Ever the penny-pincher, despite his wealth, the frugal man regularly redeemed empty bottles for cash. On this occasion, when at the bottle bank, the girl asked her captor if she could call a local church to find out their service hours. He agreed, clearly confident in his power over the teenager, and she used a payphone without him in earshot. She didn't call the church; she called her sister. In a few short minutes, she divulged some of the horrors she'd endured the past six months. Police were at the scene shortly after she hung up the phone.

Authorities were led to John Jamelske's home, where they discovered The Dungeon. The words of graffiti on the walls, the crucifix and peace signs hung on the walls, the crude makeshift bath and toilet - it all aligned with what other victims had told police. It seemed they'd snared a serial rapist.

With the girl reunited with her family, John's pleas of innocence to the police would have been comical if his crimes hadn't been so vile. He insisted that the young girl was his girlfriend and assured the police that the age gap wasn't so bad. The worst thing about the relationship, he would joke, was that she liked blue cheese, and he couldn't understand that. He told the police he wanted to be home with her that night.

Perhaps years and years of John getting away with his detestable crimes gave him a feeling he was above the law. Perhaps he presumed he had such powerful skills of manipulation and the ability to brainwash people that the police would drop their kidnapping charges and release him. Or perhaps he felt like he did no wrong in the first place. After it transpired he wouldn't be getting out of jail anytime soon, John insisted that what he did to his victims wasn't so bad. It wasn't kidnapping, he reasoned, since he didn't ask for a sum of money for the safe return of his captives. He even suggested he was doing them a favor. It seems John Jamelske's admissions did him no favors, however, since he was handed 18 years to life behind bars for five counts of first-degree kidnapping.

Even after his sentencing, regret and remorse still weren't feelings that John could muster up. If anything, he doubled down on his idea that what he'd done wasn't bad. When he was interviewed for a news program, he insisted he shouldn't be punished for his crimes. He presumed, remarkably, that he would get a fine or a few days in jail at the most for his violations. Even more surprising is the fact that his lawyers had to explain to him that kidnapping women to keep them as sex slaves in his cellar was wrong.

In the same interview, John would describe himself as "a pretty nice guy." He tried to make this clear in his trial, too, but he felt this went unheard by the judge. John was insistent that his lawyer offer the Board some evidence that would prove this: he "often provided bubble bath" to his victims.

Hopefully, a lifetime behind bars has offered deluded John a heavy dose of reality.

# An Extreme Obsession

Some true crime stories are so horribly violent or disturbing that they're difficult to read. The perpetrator is often vilified and reviled, and rightly so. Rarely is there a true crime case where the criminal is viewed with compassion or sympathy. Off the top of my head, the only well-known case I can think of like this is the story of Aileen Wuornos, a hitchhiking sex worker who killed seven of her clients. However, Wuornos' backstory was filled with sexual abuse from a young age, gross mistreatment from men her entire life, and severe neglect from every parental figure she had in her life. Her life story has evoked feelings of pity from some who followed her case, citing that she never stood a chance. It was inevitable her traumas would rear their head in awful ways, and in doing so, took the lives of seven men.

The story of Carl Tanzler is somewhat similar in the sense that his abhorrent acts of criminality were viewed with sympathy and pity. While there is no past trauma or sob story to explain his behavior, his extreme law-breaking was brought on by unrequited love, something that has been (in my opinion) unjustly romanticized in this case. Tanzler's obsession with Elena de Hoyos provoked him to do the unthinkable. If this story were not true, it would certainly serve as an imaginative basis for a twisted horror movie.

The story of Carl Tanzler is hard to categorize. Some may label his behavior as stalking. But the woman he was "stalking" was dead. Deadly obsession is perhaps a better way to put it, although it doesn't quite capture just how bizarre this story is.

This peculiar tale begins in Key West, Florida, in the spring of 1930. Known for Duval Street, a bustling area full of culture and its laid-back vibe, Key West is home to a myriad of demographics. Pastel hues cover the conch-style buildings, while the sky is almost always a clear blue.

The idyllic setting proved to be an attractive lure for many, including Cuban-American Elena de Hoyos and German-born Carl Tanzler. The pair would first cross paths at the Marine Hospital in Key West, where Elena was rushed after feeling incredibly ill. The 22-year-old was immediately noticed by the radiology technician, Tanzler. This encounter would prove to be Tanzler's descent into obsession.

Elena was quickly diagnosed with tuberculosis, and in the 30s, this bacterial infection was practically a death sentence. While Tanzler wasn't a doctor or anybody with any real medical experience, he immediately offered to do what he could to save Elena. As soon as Tanzler, in his early 50s, set eyes on young Elena, it sparked something inside of him. Perhaps as a way to keep in touch with the woman, Tanzler declared his medical knowledge would cure Elena of her infection and save her life. Of course, with tuberculosis being so deadly at the time, the Hoyos family were prepared to try anything for their beloved Elena.

Soon enough, Tanzler was turning up at the Hoyos household with various tools and implements, all to be used in an attempt to cure Elena. Potions and homemade remedies were also brought along, and the young girl endured the side effects these apparent medicines gave her with the understanding that it would save her life. Tanzler brought x-ray equipment with him, as well as equipment that would administer electric shocks to Elena.

Perhaps the reason Tanzler has been viewed with pinches of empathy is because his attempts at saving Elena seemed legitimate; he was truly obsessed with the young woman, always bringing her gifts alongside another new concoction he made in the hopes of curing her. Elena, however, didn't feel the same towards the older man. Still, gifts, "treatments," and affection were bestowed upon the sick woman right up until her death in October 1931.

His desperation wasn't enough to save Elena, and Tanzler was heartbroken. He rallied around the Hoyos family, paying for Elena's funeral and commissioning the building of a large mausoleum for his late obsession. Fueled by grief and an abundance of gratitude for Tanzler's gestures, the Hoyos family agreed to bury Elena in the tomb. What they didn't know was that Carl Tanzler would be the sole owner of the key to (what should have been) Elena's final resting place in Key West Cemetery.

Tanzler was a mainstay at Elena's grave. Every night, without fail, he was seen at her mausoleum, and he still maintained frequent contact with the Hoyos family. Oddly, Tanzler used his key to the tomb to install a phone in Elena's grave. His behavior was getting increasingly disturbing and may have contributed to his sacking from his job at the Marine Hospital, although the reasons for his dismissal are unknown. In the years following Elena's death, townsfolk were becoming suspicious of Tanzler.

The self-professed medical expert was spotted buying women's clothes and expensive perfumes. He stopped visiting Elena's grave, which had been something of a nightly ritual of his. His neighbors were being extra vigilant when curtain twitching on an evening, making sure to keep a check on Tanzler and his erratic behavior. One eagle-eyed neighbor spotted Tanzler dancing around his living room one night, swirling around the room with his less-than-enthusiastic dance partner: a life-size doll. The community put two and two together; Tanzler no longer visited Elena's grave because her corpse wasn't there. It was in his house.

It took until 1940 for this (still unfounded) talk to reach Elena's sister, Florinda. Of course, disturbed by the gossip, she sought to find out the truth. As far-fetched as it sounded, Florinda knew just how fond, for want of a better term, Tanzler was of her sister. She went to Tanzler's property, where he showed her Elena's corpse. The rumor mill had churned out the truth for once.

It didn't take long for Tanzler to confess the full story as to how he'd ended up like this. He'd broken into the mausoleum years earlier and carted Elena's embalmed body back to his property. He insisted that Elena's spirit had been visiting him and asked to be taken from her grave. Once he got her home, he spent his time preserving her corpse to prevent further decay. The desire to recreate Elena's appearance as if she were still living saw Tanzler reconstruct her face with plaster of Paris and mortician's wax. Her eyes were removed, and glass ones were put in their place. He stapled a wig to her head. He inserted a tube into her vagina, and although he didn't offer up an explanation for this, some have alluded to Tanzler being a necrophiliac. He kept his human doll on his bed as pride of place, complete with her own jewelry and signature perfumes.

Police were called, and Tanzler was charged with destroying Elena's grave and removing her body without authorization. He was evaluated by a psychiatrist but was deemed mentally well enough to stand trial. Nothing would come of this, however, since the statute of limitations for his crime had expired. Tanzler was able to walk out of the Monroe County Courthouse in Key West a free man, able to get on with his life. The public's opinion on this outcome varied, although a large number of people felt pity towards the lonely, middle-aged man who kept a human doll for company. An odd man for sure, people thought, but fueled by loneliness, not malice.

Elena's heavily modified body was displayed at a local funeral home for a short while before she would be buried for good. Over 6,000 people made their way to see Elena, perhaps more eager to see the human doll

Tanzler had created than to pay their respects. She was buried without a headstone to prevent anyone finding her and removing her from her resting place.

Unlike Aileen Wuornos, there doesn't seem to be any tragic backstory for Tanzler to help explain his adult criminal behavior. While not in the same league as Wuornos in terms of criminality, they both share outpourings of pity from people despite their repulsive acts.

Born in Germany in 1877, Tanzler emigrated to the USA from his home country in 1926, ending up in Cuba for a short time. From Cuba, he traveled to Florida, where he planned to settle in Zephyrhills. However, he eventually settled in Key West, where he met his obsession, Elena. It seems Tanzler had been waiting his whole life to meet the young woman. After all, as a young man, he claimed to have had visions of his ancestors showing him his soul mate, the only woman he would ever love. The woman in question was dark-haired and exotic-looking - not too far away from how you might describe Elena. When Tanzler first spotted her in the hospital that spring morning, he knew immediately this was the woman his visions were guiding him to.

When the young woman passed away, it seems Tanzler just couldn't accept he wouldn't ever be able to be with her again. It's important to note that there's no evidence to suggest Elena ever reciprocated Tanzler's affection. In fact, it's more likely that she gently rebuffed his advances, but still, the older man wouldn't relent. After her death, his refusal to accept her rejection resulted in him robbing her gravesite and turning her corpse into a human doll.

It's been suggested Tanzler was a necrophiliac, and the way he'd inserted a tube into the dead woman's vagina would certainly help advocate that theory. However, the post-mortem of Elena didn't show any proof of Tanzler violating her in this way, so we'll never truly know the truth about this aspect of his crimes. TV shows covering this case, particularly a late-90s episode of the program *Autopsy*, have heavily hinted that necrophilia was a big aspect of Tanzler's crimes.

While this will remain a mystery, what can't be denied is that Tanzler was a delusional man, intent on keeping his obsession with him. He truly believed he would be able to bring her back to life, and when he was caught for his crimes and Elena was taken away for good, his bizarre behavior didn't let up. Tanzler had created a "death mask" of Elena's face while he had her corpse living with him and used this plaster cast of her face to create a life-size model of her.

It's also been suggested that Tanzler was Elena's true killer, not the tuberculosis she was sick with. Rumors aren't something I'd usually delve into, but in this case, the hearsay doesn't seem too far-fetched. Apparently, construction workers renovating a cottage Tanzler once resided in found an alarming note in which he admitted to her murder. There was no repentance in the note, which read:

*She died because I gave this to her mercifully (referring to a potion he gave her of aconite)*

*Suffer no more sweet Elena, I have sent you to the angels with my golden elixir.*

Carl died on July 3, 1952, aged 75. It's been suggested that the life-size sculpture he was found with upon his death wasn't a plaster version at all but rather the real body of Elena. The rumor that ends this tragic tale suggests that Tanzler somehow managed to swap Elena's corpse with the life-sized effigy and spent his final years with her modified remains. While we'll never know if this is true or not, going by the rest of the tale, it certainly isn't an implausible idea.

# A Familiar Face

It was a sunny May day in St. Paul, Minnesota. It was Friday, and the excitement of the weekend being in sight was looming in the air. Blondie's pop-rock hit *"Call Me"* was number one in the charts and played just about everywhere. It was blasting from the speakers in Carmen's Beauty Salon as mother and daughter Mary and Elizabeth Stauffer walked out after the little girl had been treated to a new haircut. On the walk back to their car, the pair were horrified to be stopped in their tracks by a man wielding a gun. He forced the pair into the trunk of his car before taking off at speed.

Perhaps the fear of the ordeal stopped Mary from identifying the attacker. Perhaps it was because it had been a decade and a half since she last saw him. Maybe it was because she'd never really taken much notice of him in the first place. Regardless, she didn't know it yet, but the kidnapper was someone she'd already crossed paths with on multiple occasions.

The mother and child bellowed as loud as they could from the trunk of the car, begging for help, hoping a passerby would hear the commotion and stop the car and rescue them. The screaming and shouting aggravated the driver, Ming Sen Shiue, and he pulled over somewhere remote to scold the frightened pair before taping their mouths tightly shut. Ming returned to the wheel, but the silence of the trunk made him uneasy. What if they've somehow escaped? He pulled over yet again, this time somewhere less inconspicuous, and pulled open the trunk. Sure enough, mother and daughter were still there. However, little Elizabeth was no longer gagged. Irate at Mary's defiance for removing Elizabeth's tape, Ming's loud fury attracted attention from boys playing in the nearby park.

The boys walked up to the commotion, and little Jason Wilkman had a peek inside the open trunk. He gasped at what he saw, but before he could run and get help, Ming bear-hugged the six-year-old and flung him in the boot with the other captives. The other boy managed to escape the clutches of the kidnapper and raced as fast as he could to safety.

However, Jason had no place in Ming's nefarious plans. He was going to ruin everything he'd been planning for so long.

After driving north for a short while, Ming dragged the terrified boy from the trunk and began pummeling him with a metal bar. The boy's tiny body, bloodied and broken, was dumped in the woods near Carlos Avery State Wildlife Park. There was no chance he could survive such a brutal attack.

Ming resumed his place behind the wheel and took his two hostages to his house in Roseville. He bundled the pair from the car and locked them in his 4-foot-tall closet.

That night, he removed Mary from the closet and tethered her to some furniture. It was at this point he revealed his identity and told her that he was her math student years prior. After the revelation, he proceeded to rape the woman repeatedly. Ming also used a video camera to record much of the abuse, as well as conversations he had with Mary over the course of a few weeks. One conversation saw the kidnapper explain to Mary that a low grade she gave him for a math test years earlier meant he couldn't get into college. Because of this, he told her, he was drafted into the Vietnam War, during which time he was a prisoner of war. However, Ming never let the truth get in the way of a good story - none of this was true.

Days passed as the mother and daughter were held captive. Often, Ming would keep them separate, and he was verbally and emotionally abusive, on top of being extremely violent. As well as raping Mary on a daily basis, he told her he'd kill her husband and son if she ever tried to escape. She took his threats at face value. After all, she'd witnessed Ming bludgeon a little boy to death with no remorse or reason. She believed him when he told her that her son would meet the same fate if she stepped out of line. Day after day, the horrific routine didn't relent: Ming would lock the pair away in cramped confinement until he returned home from working at the electronics store he owned. Then, he'd unlock the captives and rape and abuse for hours on end. He tried to suffocate little Elizabeth at one point and only stopped when Mary kissed him. The unpredictability of Ming meant neither mother nor child knew if they were going to make it to the end of each day.

But what would cause Ming to feel such venom towards Mary Stauffer that he wanted to track her down a decade and a half after she taught him algebra?

Like a lot of criminals do, Ming presented troubling behavior as a child. He always had to be right, his mother said, and couldn't abide being told he was wrong. He was violent back then, too, beating his siblings for no good reason other than he wanted to. His abusive behavior towards his siblings didn't stop at adolescence; Ming lashed out at them as an adult, too. He was arrested several times as a troublesome teen, even having to go to therapy after being found out as the culprit for several arsons. Downright fearful of her son, Ming's mother couldn't discipline him. He got away with whatever wickedness he wished to carry out without any repercussions. Although I can't quite understand the analogy, Ming's mother said he was like a dog because he had "no feelings."

However, it seems this can't have been true. He did have feelings, albeit macabre, violent ones. He was obsessed with his math teacher, Mary Stauffer. Ming was utterly infatuated with the older woman, even writing sexual stories about her. Eventually, the stories of consensual sex turned more sinister. Soon, Ming was writing about Mary's rape. That soon escalated into gang rape. It got to a point where these horrific stories no longer satisfied the teenager, and he began plotting to carry these acts out on Mary in real life. He just needed to kidnap her first.

For 15 years, Ming never gave up on his desire to make his fiction a reality. In fact, in 1975, the obsessed 25-year-old thought he'd finally located his obsession's home. He'd waited years for this, and he couldn't wait to break in and take what he'd been fantasizing over for so long. Armed with a gun, Ming broke into the house, only to find a couple he'd never met living there. It turned out these people were Mary's in-laws. When he found out his mistake, he didn't flee. He tied the couple up and flung them to the floor. Fearfully, they heeded Ming's threat: don't go to the police, or you'll be killed. The break-in and assault remained unreported, and Ming was free for another five years to stalk Mary.

This brings us back to May 1980. Mary and Elizabeth are locked in the closet. Ming is at his shop. They'd lost count, but the pair had been kept captive for 53 days by this point. Mary's grit, determination, and motherly instincts had kept the pair alive this far. But how much longer could they go on? Ming was unstable, and his mood and behavior could change at any given moment. Mary tinkered with the hinges on the wardrobe door while her abductor was at work, hoping the door would fall off and free the pair to call for help. Eventually, the hinge broke, and Mary, along with Elizabeth, who was tied to her, raced to the phone to call the police. The police told the pair to stay where they were; help was on the way.

Sure enough, sirens and flashing lights filled the streets, and Ming's house was surrounded by police cars. One officer spotted something strange out of the corner of his eye, though: someone huddled up behind a parked car, clearly hiding. He drew his gun and walked towards the suspicious figure. He told them to show themselves, and the figure obliged. It was Mary, with Elizabeth by her side. They were too fearful to remain in the house with Ming due home at any moment. The terrified pair were now safe if severely traumatized by the ordeal they'd been through.

It wasn't just Mary and Elizabeth who'd endured Ming's mindless violence. Jason Wilkman's young friend had reported to police that his buddy had been kidnapped by a strange man, but that was as much information as the boy could provide. Mary would deliver the news to police that Jason was also a captive of Ming's, but he was cruelly bludgeoned to death over a month earlier. She could, however, give his family the closure they sought by offering up the painful news.

Police headed to Ming's shop to arrest him. He was cuffed and thrown into the back of the police car, likely in a more humane way than he offered Mary and Elizabeth when he flung them into his car trunk.

Still, Ming wouldn't repent while behind bars. Quite the opposite, in fact. He offered another prisoner, Richard Green, $50,000 to kill Mary and Elizabeth. Their deaths would prevent them from identifying and testifying against him in court. The murderer didn't bank on Green taking this information straight to the FBI, scuppering his evil plot before it began. It seemed like the odds were stacked heavily against Ming, and he had no way out of the situation he'd gotten himself into, but his villainous behavior still managed to rear its ugly head while the trial was ongoing.

The case required two trials. One for Jason's murder, the other for Mary and Elizabeth's kidnapping and the repeated rape of Mary. This was because Ming had taken the pair over state lines when he committed his crimes. It also meant Mary had to testify at both trials, enduring two exhausting rehashes of her traumatic ordeal. The second trial saw Ming expose his true colors and throw in some theatrics before his sentencing.

Somehow, the murderer had managed to sneak a knife into the courtroom. As soon as he saw an opportunity to get close enough to Mary, who was brave enough to face not just one but two trials against her rapist, he slashed her face with the knife. He managed to get so close to her that the depth of the cut caused the woman to require 62 stitches. While slashing Mary's face, he issued a threat: should he ever be freed, he'd kill her and Elizabeth.

The unrepentant man was handed 40 years in jail for the murder of Jason. He was given 30 to life for the rapes and kidnapping.

Can someone so unapologetic and brazen about their crimes ever truly be regretful for their behavior?

Fast forward to 2010, and that's just what Ming claimed to be. During a parole hearing, Ming expressed sorrow for his actions and asked for his victims' forgiveness. At the risk of sounding pessimistic, I'm always bemused at the amount of criminals who profess repentance and remorse at the same hearing used to decide if they're eligible to be freed into society.

This same self-condemnation is almost always notably absent in the years prior. In fact, Ming was diagnosed as having a sexual psychopathic personality while in jail. He didn't take up the offer of sex offender treatment, however. His parole request was denied. Still, there is a chance he may one day be free to roam the streets, although his requests have been continually denied this far.

I wonder how someone would ever bounce back from a traumatic event like this. There's no denial; it's life-altering. But Mary, who is incredibly private, feels her faith has helped her through. She even prays for her rapist. Elizabeth, who now has a family of her own, insists he didn't ruin their lives. "He ruined *his* life," she states, clearly still owning the same resilience that kept her alive while being held captive in 1980.

# If You Loved Me, You'd Do This For Me

The story of Cinnamon Brown, who was just 14 years old when her hellish tale began, is a case that is driven by greed and lust, ultimately ending in murder and betrayal. In the spring of 1985, the teenager found herself thrust into the justice system for a horrific killing she was accused of carrying out. The case should have been pretty open and shut since Cinnamon admitted to the crime, the callous shooting of Linda Brown, her stepmother. However, this crime wasn't as black and white as it initially appeared, and it seemed there was more than just one victim in this sad story: Cinnamon herself.

The affluent city of Garden Grove is located in Orange County, California. The family-oriented area, famous for its annual Strawberry Festival, is considered a relatively safe place to live. But, like most suburban crime in places like this, the most horrific crimes are carried out behind closed doors. On the outside, the Brown family looked like the picture-perfect household. However, the opposite was true.

On March 19, 1985, David Brown, exasperated by his wife and daughter's incessant arguing, left the family home to get some peace and remove himself from the shouting and animosity. He stayed out until late, hoping to return to a calmer environment. What he returned to, however, was far from harmonious. Heading up to bed, he was greeted with an awfully bloody sight. His wife, Linda, was strewn across the bed with gunshots pumped into her chest. David called the police, who arrived alongside an ambulance that rushed the dying woman to Fountain Valley Regional Hospital.

Sadly, 23-year-old Linda Brown was pronounced dead almost as soon as she arrived at the hospital.

David was in a state of shock at the horror he'd arrived home to, refusing to enter the marital bedroom, clearly and understandably distressed by the act of violence carried out on his wife. Although David was out at the time of the murder, there was someone in the house during the vicious attack who could offer up some critical evidence - or possibly even be the culprit of the crime.

Police began searching for Cinnamon, who was absent from her bed and nowhere to be found in the house. She hadn't got too far, though; police found her huddled up behind the doghouse in the yard. The state they found her in was a disturbing sight for the officers. The teenager was covered in her own vomit, barely coherent, and clutching a ribbon-tied note. "Dear God," the note began, "please forgive me. I didn't mean to hurt her." The 14-year-old was bundled up and swiftly arrested for her stepmother's murder.

Although Cinnamon was clearly frightened, nervous, and overwhelmed by the ordeal, she'd quickly confessed to the murder of Linda, so police had no choice but to charge her and take the case to trial. When in court, Cinnamon could remember very little about the night of the murder, seeming to forget quite a lot about the evening in question. The police were already skeptical about her version of events, but the teen assured them that she had shot her stepmother and was indeed the murderer. There was no evidence to suggest otherwise, either. Still, it was agreed that Cinnamon would plead not guilty due to insanity.

The trial saw the teen painted as a callous killer who shot her stepmother in cold blood after an argument. The court heard how Linda had threatened to throw Cinnamon out of the house, which angered the girl into loading a gun and shooting Linda as she slept. Cinnamon was also labeled as being depressed, moody, and angry, particularly in the weeks leading up to the shooting. David Brown would testify against his daughter, telling the court about her perpetually low moods and desire to kill herself. David claimed that just the night prior to Linda's murder, he had shown his daughter how to shoot a gun properly. Her newfound knowledge of guns coupled with her anger towards her stepmother, had created a perfect storm for the tragic event of Linda's murder to occur.

Notably quiet throughout the trial, Cinnamon expressed her shock at being found guilty of first-degree murder. "I don't understand," she gasped as the judge read out the verdict. Confused and afraid, Cinnamon still had to endure the sentencing process, which would see her defense team argue that the young girl wasn't in her right mind at the time of the shooting. Manuela Brown, Cinnamon's grandmother, told the court that her granddaughter had imaginary friends, perhaps as a result of her depression.

Cinnamon was handed 27 years behind bars, initially being placed with the California Youth Authority due to her age.

But not everyone took Cinnamon's admission of guilt at face value. Her mother, Brenda Sands, couldn't grasp how her daughter could have committed such a callous act of violence, telling the press that her baby was sweet and polite, a stark contrast from the moody, angry young girl the trial - and her own father - had presented her as.

While his daughter was doing her best to acclimatize herself to prison life, David Brown had seemingly skipped the grieving process and was living a notably lavish lifestyle. The widower had cashed in $835,000 from his deceased wife's life insurance, of which some of the policies had been taken out just weeks prior to her murder. David had also sought comfort, it seemed, in the arms of his sister-in-law, Linda's 17-year-old sister, Patti. Perhaps if the authorities knew of these facts, along with David's overbearing and controlling nature, they'd have taken a second look at Cinnamon's confession. So dominating and commanding, in fact, he made Patti wear a beeper at all times to ensure she wouldn't stray. Over time, these facts trickled their way into the Orange County Sheriff's Department.

Years passed, and Cinnamon remained behind bars, no doubt still wondering where it all went wrong. She had no clue her father was thriving in the outside world, let alone that he'd married his late wife's sister. Maybe, authorities thought, if Cinnamon knew exactly what was going on in the outside world, she'd have a little more information to tell them about what really went on during that fateful night in 1985. Police told the teenager how her father was living an opulent lifestyle while she was isolated from the world, buying up half-a-million-dollar homes in the OC, all courtesy of Linda Brown's life insurance. Oh, and *didn't she know*? He'd married Linda's younger sister, too.

This didn't go down well with Cinnamon. The truth spurted out of her, fueled by anger and betrayal.

"Girls, it has to be done tonight," David insisted to the two girls as he woke them from their slumber. Cinnamon and Patti sat up in their beds, knowing full well what David was alluding to. Patti had been staying with her sister, Linda, while covertly having an affair with David. Any hesitation on the girls' part was cut dead, with David repeating the same line they'd heard for months: *If you loved me, you'd do this for me.*

The girls were prepped quickly before heeding David's orders. Just like she was told, Cinnamon pumped bullets into Linda's sleeping body. She raced out of the now-bloodied bedroom, but the victim was still alive; she was groaning at least. Another shot of the .38 caliber into the blanket silenced the pained noises but replaced them with the gurgling sounds of gasping for air. Linda Brown, mother of a 7-month-old baby girl, eventually succumbed to the bullet wounds in her chest. David would go on to act like the heartbroken husband when, in reality, he'd been readying his daughter for this moment for months.

Still, it was Cinnamon's word against her father's, who most likely wouldn't drop the facade and admit to orchestrating his ex-wife's murder. After all, if you looked a little deeper into David's past, he wasn't exactly trustworthy or decent.

In his mid-20s, he began dating Pam Bailey, a teenager who lived just down the road from him. He'd used his gift of the gab, alongside a lie that he had terminal cancer, to gain her interest and pity. The empathic young girl would soon become his lover, although David soon set his sights on her sister Linda, aged just 13. The pair would elope to Vegas when Linda was 17, but she still needed her mother's written approval for the marriage to be official. Linda's brother would later say of David, "He was always a guy who liked having younger girls, little girls."

David would go on to have a child with Linda, while also bringing his daughter from another marriage into the household. A few years prior to this, Linda's sister Patti Bailey also joined the Brown household at age 11, around the same age she would be when David began his illicit grooming of her. He escalated from inviting her to sit on his knee to tell her what a good girl she was to inappropriate touching of the youngster under the guise of making her "a lady." Cinnamon even walked in on Patti kissing her father at one point, but nothing came of it. Perhaps David's smooth-talking convinced her it wasn't what it looked like, or perhaps she knew what was going on but believed she was powerless to stop it.

Patti, much like Cinnamon, had an unstable upbringing much of her childhood. Prior to moving in with the Browns, the pair were often unsure when they'd get their next meal. The lure of regular meals, new clothes, and a warm roof over their heads was enough to entice the young girls to live with David and Linda. Perhaps out of gratitude, the girls found themselves devoted to David and can go some way in explaining why they followed his murderous plan until the end.

Over the course of the following two years, David began telling Patti about how her sister was trying to take over his lucrative business. Data Recovery Inc. was David's brain-child, and he was earning quite a handsome income in the IT industry. But that could all be taken away if Linda got her way, David would confide in his young victim. Linda and her brother Alan would stop at nothing to take over the thriving IT company, even if it meant getting rid of David completely. Patti, young and naïve, believed what she was hearing: her sister was an evil, manipulative woman who was going to not only destroy everything David had worked for but also demolish the creature comforts she'd become accustomed to. Soon, David was telling Cinnamon the same: his money-hungry wife was out to get him.

Initially, Cinnamon was diplomatic. *Just get a divorce*, she suggested. *Leave Linda if she's trying to take your business away from you.* David scoffed at this idea, reminding Cinnamon that alimony would ruin him; plus Linda knew all of his business secrets. She would launch a competitor that would drive them into bankruptcy. The idea that the cushy life they were living would be ruined by an evil gold digger soon became a real threat for the two young girls.

David's poison had seeped into the girls' minds so much that Patti even believed she overheard her sister plotting David's demise on the phone, abruptly ending the conversation when she became aware Patti was around.

In the months that followed, David, Cinnamon, and Patti all bounced ideas off each other. How Linda should die, when, and what weapons ought to be used... would a toaster in the bath be enough to kill her? How about a hit-and-run? One thing was made clear from the off:

David wouldn't be the one to commit the murder. He was too sick, he would say, as he reached into his medicine cabinet and selected a bottle of pills from the array of medications.

David suggested a murder-suicide idea. He made the girls write goodbye notes and showed them how to make a fake deadly cocktail to take after the murder. While Patti had shown willingness in the beginning, the idea of killing her older sister began to make her feel uneasy. Cinnamon would have to do David's dirty work, it was decided. After all, she was 14, too young to get into trouble. David assured his daughter that she would survive the suicide attempt and, after being declared mentally unwell, would be sent home.

When Cinnamon was woken by her father to carry out the murder, he handed her the carefully wrapped .38 gun and plied her with painkillers. The teenager followed her father's instructions and afterward fled in panic and distress to the dog house outside.

For three years, the teenager had kept all of this from the authorities. Still, David denied what his daughter had told the police, but a tape recording would expose him for what he truly was. Just weeks before he was arrested for orchestrating Linda's murder, he was taped while speaking with his daughter. The incriminating conversation included David pleading with Cinnamon to not tell the police what really happened, insisting he'd never survive in prison.

That was all the police needed to make an arrest. Still, it seemed like David hadn't learned his lesson about openly divulging too much information. While behind bars, he told an undercover officer that he'd pay her to tell authorities that Patti had confessed that her and Cinnamon's story was fabricated. He would make it worth her while, he promised, while reminding her that's how he got ahead in life: by taking care of people. His comment was as ironic as it was laughable.

Then there was another elaborate scheme David cooked up while behind bars prior to his trial. He attempted to pay a hitman tens of thousands of dollars to kill Patti alongside some of the prosecution staff. Why would an innocent man go to such lengths to thwart his prosecution?

It turns out the jury asked themselves the same question and convicted David of choreographing his wife's murder. In June 1990, his guilty verdict was read out, although David still maintains his innocence. He accused the prosecution of having blood on their hands, insisting that Patti and Cinnamon were the true killers - and would most certainly kill again.

David's prediction never came true. Cinnamon was released in 1992 and hasn't been in trouble with the law since. Patti served a few years behind bars for her role in the murder, but she's avoided being on the police radar since her release, too.

Not much is known about Cinnamon or what she's up to now. You can imagine the trauma of being betrayed and manipulated to such an extent by your own father would have had heavy implications on your perception and ability to trust. Factor in that Cinnamon lost her adolescence to the isolation of the California Youth Authority, she would have had the task of integrating herself into a society without the foundation of friends, family, or any support network she could trust.

David is still behind bars, where he'll be until he dies.

# You'll Find My Footprint On My Dad

To imagine a 15-year-old girl murdering anyone is difficult, much less being capable of killing two people. To make this scenario even darker, one of the murder victims in the case I'm about to cover is the young culprit's father. However far-fetched it may sound, this macabre situation is the reality for Lorraine Thorpe, a British woman - a teenager at the time of the crimes - who took part in two torture killings with her partner, Paul Clarke. Although I use the term "partner" here, it's important to note that Clarke was in his 40s while he allegedly "courted" Lorraine. While there was undoubtedly an uneven power dynamic in this relationship, the idea that Clarke coerced or forced his young partner in crime to commit these murders alongside him has been disproven. On the contrary, evidence has suggested that Lorraine Thorpe, despite her age, was manipulative and violent.

Born in 1994 in the town of Ipswich, England, Lorraine grew up surrounded by poverty and a culture of street drinking. She was often privy to drunken violence and the antisocial behaviors of the adults she was in the care of. Her father had custody of his young daughter, although social services quickly got involved when they caught wind of her less-than-ideal living circumstances. Often, Lorraine and her father, Desmond, would have to live in tents or in some of the squalid properties of the local alcoholics. This unstable lifestyle was made more traumatic for a young Lorraine as she witnessed her dad and his associates engage in intoxicated fights and steal from one another to buy booze.

Social services tried to offer Lorraine some respite from this lifestyle, even placing her in a special school to keep track of her whereabouts. However, no matter what social services did to intervene, Lorraine always found a way to make it back to her father. It was all she knew, and despite the fact she was essentially her dad's carer - helping him up from drunken stupors, making sure he got home safe, ensuring the pair ate - she never failed to make it back to him.

While it wasn't ideal, it was home for Lorraine, and she was unable to settle anywhere other than with her father. Perhaps she was afraid of what kind of state he'd be in without her there to keep an eye on him, or maybe she felt an overwhelming urge to rebel from the structured lifestyle social services tried to offer her; whatever her reason for returning to the run-down estate she grew up on, there's no denying there was nothing good for a wayward teenager there.

It was through her father's drinking circle that Lorraine met Paul Clarke in 2009. In his 40s, alcoholic Clarke was known as somewhat of a dominating figure among the group, with some sources referring to him as the "ringleader." It wasn't long before Clarke set his sights on the vulnerable teenager, and soon Lorraine would spend most of her time with the older man. Their days were spent much the same as the last: drinking, visiting one another's council flats, engaging in a verbal or physical altercation, and then repeating it all again the following day. It was obvious Lorraine's situation wasn't going to end well, but nobody could predict just how terrible and violent things would become.

Another regular member of the drinking group was Rosalyn Hunt. Rosie, as she was known to friends and family, was vulnerable, as most of the group were, but the 41-year-old woman was especially so. Other members of the community would use Rosalyn's flat as a place to crash or drink, often without her permission. Even if she said no to letting people enter her property, it's unlikely they'd have heeded her anyhow. They took advantage of her passive nature, and she was also afraid of certain group members, causing her to sometimes not return to her own home. This was the case in August 2009, when she had a particularly nasty falling out with Paul Clarke.

The specifics are unclear, but Rosalyn was apparently accused by Clarke of kicking his dog when it attacked a child. He was furious enough for her to refuse to go back to her own home, but she was quickly convinced to head back by Lorraine. She didn't know it, but Rosalyn was walking back to her death. Heartbreakingly, it would be a prolonged death, taking the woman days to die from the horrific torture inflicted upon her.

Lorraine coaxed the vulnerable woman into Clarke's property, which began two days of horrific violence on Rosalyn. The duo began kicking and punching the woman, with no amount of pleading or crying from Rosalyn stopping the teenager and older man from relentlessly assaulting her. The violence would only escalate from there.

One or both of the attackers used a cheese grater on Rosalyn's face. A chain dog lead was used as a whip. Her hair was set alight. At one point, the attackers threatened to slice the victim's face with an electric fan which had its guard removed. Salt was poured into open wounds to amplify her suffering. She was forced to get inside a suitcase, which was then zipped shut. The emotional and physical torture was unwavering, and for two days, Rosalyn was held hostage at Clarke's property. Unbelievably, other members of the drinking community dropped by while the woman was there, witnessing some of the sickening violence first-hand. Some of the people who were at Clarke's place while Rosalyn was being beaten are suggested to have joined in on the violence, but this theory can't be proven.

Lorraine and Clarke, realizing that Rosalyn couldn't stay at his place much longer, waited until the dark of night before frog-marching her back to her own place. There was no respite for the bloodied and beaten woman here, though; the vicious duo continued their diabolical attack on the woman. She succumbed to her many, many injuries here and was left to die on her bed, covered in dried blood, full of purple bruises, with nine broken ribs and her face significantly swollen.

With their punching bag no longer of any use, Lorraine and Clarke left Rosalyn's property and continued with their usual day-to-day routine. However, they weren't exactly quiet about the atrocious acts they'd just engaged in, and Lorraine's father, Desmond, overheard the pair discussing what they'd done to Rosalyn. The risk of the pair getting sent to jail for the crime had just increased tenfold - they now had a witness who could testify that he'd heard the murderous duo talking about killing Rosalyn. It was decided - he had to be silenced.

While his death wasn't as prolonged as the victim before him, there's no doubt Desmond suffered. He was all too aware that his daughter and Clarke wanted to end his life as they held a cushion over his face, waiting for him to stop flailing his arms and legs. While he struggled, Lorraine kicked her father and stamped on his head. They left his frail body on the floor of his flat to be discovered by one of Desmond's friends.

When news of his death broke, it was particularly alarming for the community since mere hours prior to the discovery of Desmond's body, another murder case had been reported just around the corner: that of Rosalyn Hunt.

It didn't take long for the police to put the pieces of the macabre puzzle together. Clarke and Lorraine were arrested, although they denied the charges against them. Despite their protests of innocence, they couldn't fight off the piles of evidence heaped against them. Despite denying his murder, Lorraine did confess to police that they'd find her footprints on her father's head.

Throughout their trial, neither culprit would stand and give evidence. The prosecution offered up a damning witness testimony from one of Lorraine's friends, to whom she'd confessed to being a murderer. There was also one of Lorraine's fellow inmates who testified against her, telling the jury about a conversation she'd had with her where she'd spoken about killing her dad.

On August 3, 2010, the pair were convicted of the double murder, and Clarke was handed life behind bars. Lorraine, however, had her sentencing delayed for two months, perhaps due to her young age. Still, in October 2010, she was given life imprisonment with a minimum of 14 years.

There are still lots of unanswered questions as to why these murders took place. There really wasn't any motive offered up by the killers, and police were unable to pinpoint a motive that made much sense. The torture and murder of Rosalyn were most difficult to comprehend - she hadn't done anything to provoke being attacked, much less have such aggressive and vicious violence inflicted upon her. The judge who sentenced Lorraine noted that the teenager was keen to impress the older man, who she viewed as a "role model," but emphasized that she was far from being remorseful for her part in the murders. He felt as though while Lorraine idolized Clarke, she wasn't under his influence and described her as being "wily, manipulative, and stubborn." She seemed to relish in the violence, particularly when recounting the tale to a friend about how she stamped on Rosalyn's head.

There was also a lesser-covered aspect of the case: the possible involvement of a third participant in the murder of Rosalyn. A man named John Grimwood was arrested along with the pair. He was part of the street drinking scene and had been at Clarke's and Rosalyn's properties around the time of the murders. In fact, some witnesses testified that they'd seen Grimwood being violent towards Rosalyn while she was being held at Clarke's property. However, there was insufficient evidence to convict him, so he was set free. A year after his release, he'd find himself back in the dock, this time for killing his girlfriend.

After Grimwood was cleared of Rosalyn's murder, he returned to Ipswich to his girlfriend, Alison Studd. Like a lot of the people in the area, she struggled with alcohol and substance abuse, rendering her vulnerable to those who chose to exploit her. Witnesses would tell how they often spotted Alison with bust lips and black eyes at the hands of her boyfriend.

In January 2001, Grimwood attacked a woman on the street, stabbing her multiple times. The victim begged her attacker to stop, questioning him why he was punching her. She didn't realize that he had a knife in his hands, and she thought he was pummeling her with his fists. It was only when her friend, who was standing nearby, spotted the attack and shouted, "Run! He's stabbing you!" that the woman understood the severity of her attack. Luckily, she survived the ordeal after a stint in intensive care, but Grimwood's partner, Alison, wouldn't be so fortunate later that day.

After the attack, he returned home, where an argument ensued with Alison, and with the same knife used on his previous victim, he slashed his girlfriend below the knee, cutting a vein. It was a main artery, and Alison Studd sadly and senselessly bled to death. He was handed 20 years in jail for murder. While he was cleared of any participation in Rosalyn Hunt's murder, the woman who survived his knife attack did question why he was ever released since he had a lengthy record of such violence. His subsequent arrest for another woman's murder perhaps has people second-guessing his participation in the torture-murder a year prior.

When Lorraine Thorpe was sentenced, she was given the moniker "Britain's Youngest Female Double Killer", a title that is hopefully not surpassed anytime soon.

Both killers appealed against their sentences, but these appeals were quickly shut down. After four years in jail, Paul Clarke was found dead in his cell. His death was ruled a suicide.

Lorraine is eligible to be released in 2024. She will be 30 years old.

# Love Is Blind

No tale of love is straightforward. There are ups, downs, and the mundane contentment in between. While many of us enjoy reading tales of passion, the love story, for want of a better phrase, of Burt and Linda Pugach seems too twisted to be true.

He chased her, and she was flattered, but he didn't do right by her. When she called off their romance after finding out about his indiscretions, Burt dealt with the rejection by hiring people to blind her. You'd think this tragic story would end there, but it doesn't; Linda ended up marrying Burt after he orchestrated the life-altering attack on her.

Linda Riss was barely in her 20s when she met the man who would go on to maim her. She was a picture of youth, with flawless, dewy skin, big dark brown eyes, and even bigger dark brown hair. Burt, a successful lawyer in his 30s, was instantly smitten. It didn't take long for his seeming adoration to turn into a dangerous obsession, however.

It was 1956 when Burt spotted an attractive brunette walking through the local park and immediately decided to introduce himself to her. The young woman was initially hesitant to reciprocate Burt's advances, but the attraction was there. It helped that he had money, something Linda's family had done without during the Great Depression. Burt pretended he recognized the petite woman, asking if she'd been an actress in one of his films. Of course, he knew she'd never been involved in any of his movies, but he wanted to assert his wealth and luxurious lifestyle straight away.

His wallet was full. He drove an impressive car, had a private plane, and more money than he knew what to do with. When Linda got home from her chance encounter with the wealthy man who asked her out on a date, she found roses awaiting her. He was undeniably smooth.

As the courtship evolved, Linda would come to learn that her boyfriend was jealous and controlling. He made it clear he didn't want Linda to have male friends. He'd badger her about sleeping together, although Linda never gave into the pressure. Burt was paranoid that his young girlfriend was cheating on him, so much so that he booked Linda an appointment with the doctor who would confirm to him she was still a virgin. It was a lot for the young woman to deal with, but she endured Burt's constant need for reassurance. Perhaps it had something to do with Linda's self-esteem, or lack of it, that saw her cave to most of Burt's often unreasonable demands. Not having much in the way of confidence, Linda was flattered that she was so desired by Burt, and when he asked her to marry him, she said yes.

The wedding planning was all systems go for the newly engaged couple when a phone call came through that was like a punch in the gut for Linda. It was Burt's wife, Francine, explaining that she was married to the serial cheat. Not only that, they had a daughter together. Francine warned Linda that she'd never divorce Burt, perhaps because she was the sole carer for their daughter, who had learning difficulties, and was worried about what would become of the child without the financial support.

After the dizzying phone call, Linda immediately called Burt.

He confessed it was true and promised Linda that he'd divorce his wife as quickly as possible. Linda didn't want to speak to Burt until his divorce was finalized, and he agreed to this stipulation, so it was a surprise when he turned up at her doorstep the following day. Surely he couldn't have the papers already? It turned out he did, and he handed the divorce documents to Linda with a grin on his face. She may have been young, but she certainly wasn't dumb: Linda made sure to note down the divorce number from the papers and made inquiries to confirm it was legitimate. It wasn't.

The lie after lie was enough for Linda to cut contact with Burt, but he was incensed by the rejection. He wasn't used to hearing the word "no," so when Linda was adamant in her decision to end things, he refused to accept it. He sent gifts to her door, poured his heart out in several letters, and even called her friends as a way to speak to her.

While this was going on, Burt was also having trouble with his career. The law firm he owned was under scrutiny by the police for illegal practices, which further added to Burt's desperate state. It seemed like everything was crumbling around him, and he was contemplating ending things. His letters to Linda went from soft and apologetic to outright threatening. One letter warned her that if she wouldn't be with him, he'd never allow her to be with anybody. In hindsight, this threat becomes especially chilling. On one occasion, he took his gun and parked up outside her East Bronx apartment, mustering up the will to shoot. In the end, he drove off, but his desire to hurt Linda didn't disappear.

On a warm June day in 1959, Linda's doorbell rang. She asked her mother to see to the caller, but the men at the door told her there was a package that they needed to hand to Linda. She headed to the door, tying her thick brown hair up, exposing her face. Lye was tossed toward her as she met with the caller, who raced off, leaving Linda shrieking in the doorway.

She lost her hair. She lost most of her sight. She knew who was behind this and told the police as much. It didn't take them long to arrest Burt and apprehend the three men involved in the attack. In 1961, Burt was handed three decades behind bars for the heinous crime. He served less than half that time.

While Burt was in prison, Linda did her best to avoid letting the life-changing attack ruin what ought to have been some of the best years of her life. She traveled, headed to Europe with some friends, and dabbled in holiday romances and flirtationships. She still had a small amount of sight left at this point, and she enjoyed dancing and meeting new people. She made sure to always wear a big pair of sunglasses, however, as she was unsure how people would react to her eyes. The once big, brown orbs were now a bluish hue. This insecurity lasted until she met a man who she thought could have been a potential suitor. He fell head over heels for her and even asked her to marry him. Then, she met up with him without the black sunglasses she used to hide her eyes. She never heard from him again. Linda's attempt at becoming confident about who she was had fallen flat. She was beyond upset, and her self-esteem had been obliterated.

She came back to the States and resumed her life. She found that Burt hadn't forgotten about her. He'd sent letters proclaiming his love for her, insisting that she'd never find anyone who'd love her like he did. He even referred to himself as her husband in the letters. In the end, he resorted to speaking to his lawyer, requesting that he reach out to Linda and ask if Burt could do anything for her. It turns out there was: Linda needed money. Burt sent her installments here and there to make sure she didn't want for anything.

Burt was released in 1974, 14 years into his 30-year sentence. His good behavior got him out early, and he again began his pursuit of Linda. She was in police protection, however, but that didn't stop her former lover from his relentless chasing. Linda's friends were worried about her. She was now in her late 30s, and they considered how she might look after herself as she got older. He really seemed to love her, they said. Linda wasn't sure, but she also wasn't sure anybody else might want her, describing herself as "damaged merchandise." She met with Burt, and the pair married that same year.

Linda would later say she'd never held a high opinion of herself, a tragic lack of self-worth that you may opine contributed to her relenting and marrying Burt after everything he'd done to her. She thought that growing up without a father had impacted the way she felt about herself, and she didn't speak of her younger self with much praise.

However, as she got older, it seemed she adjusted to her new way of living. She embraced the dark sunglasses she always wore, enjoying the air of mystique it gave her. Although she would eventually go completely blind, she only needed to touch the clothes in her wardrobe to know what color they were. She found her strength as she got older with Burt but never spoke about the attack with him. She felt it would be unfair to confront him about that after marrying him. Burt would later say his decision to have Linda attacked was brought on by the pressure of being summoned to court over illegal going on at his firm.

Burt worked as a paralegal after being released from prison, a role that offered husband and wife a comfortable life together. Still, Burt wasn't a reliable husband in other aspects. His wandering eye was a constant, and he cheated on Linda more times than he could recollect. He argued that some people's vices are drugs or too much wine... His vice was women. With Linda unable to see, Burt was able to wander freely without the prospect of being caught by his wife. Still, she knew what her husband was like and chalked the cheating up to "something men do."

Evangeline Borga was one of Burt's conquests, his Filipino secretary, who eventually had Burt arrested for harassment. His mistress claimed the older man-made threats to blind her as he had with Linda. She also said that he'd told her he would divorce Linda if she agreed to marry him. Burt didn't deny this; in fact, he admitted to it but said it was an outright lie to his mistress, the same one he'd told Linda decades earlier. He was taken to court, and the charismatic man represented himself. He was defended by Linda, insisting her husband did nothing except have an extramarital affair. After all, do all wives truly know what their husband gets up to, Linda asked the press.

Burt and Linda lived together until her death in January 2013. For a while, Burt lived alone until he struck up a conversation with a woman in a New York deli in 2016. The woman was married, but by some newspaper reports, Burt was enthralled by her and eventually moved in with her and her husband. He began changing his will frequently, leaving differing amounts - large amounts - to his new friend. However, this concerned Burt's longtime friends, as he cut off the foundation his late wife set up to help the visually impaired. He was leaving more and more to a woman who described herself as his "caregiver." Those close to Burt stressed that he would never amend his will to take Linda's charity out of it, insinuating that the older man was being manipulated. Upon Burt's death in 2020, it was revealed he'd left his friend and her husband $15 million.

This story is atypical of most true crime tales. The perpetrator was granted forgiveness from the victim, although it's hard to gauge if he'd ever truly been sorry enough for that. The victim married the man who'd tried to ruin her life forever. More than this, she dedicated the rest of her life to him. This tale, if you delve underneath the surface, offers more than a wild "crime of passion" story. It's ingrained with toxicity, coercive behaviors, helplessness, and codependency. A sad case all around, and whether justice was truly served or the victim was properly protected, could be up for debate.

# Terror At Tiede Cabin

Von Lester Taylor and Edward Steven Deli were criminals with lengthy rap sheets. Taylor had been arrested for burglary, robbery, and assault, while Deli had a history of drug charges. The pair were living in a halfway house in Utah when the parolees had been trusted to take themselves job-hunting, but they went on the run instead. The duo had been at large for just over a week when they happened across a cozy-looking cabin in the woods. The dangerous pair found what they'd been looking for: a place to offer food, shelter, and a family to terrorize.

Meanwhile, with Christmas soon approaching, the Tiede family were readying to gather at their cabin in the snowy Utah mountains. Sixteen-year-old Trish Tiede and her 20-year-old sister Linae were excited to spend the festive season in the remote mountains with their mother Kaye, grandmother Beth, and dad Rolf. They were to be joined by various members of their extended family made up of cousins, aunts, and uncles. In preparation for the festive family gathering, stockings were hung over the mantlepiece, tinsel and decorations filled the rooms, and the fridge was filled with plentiful food to ensure nobody went hungry while at the property the family called "Tiede's Tranquility."

The cabin was well out of the way, with the nearest road two miles away. This meant the only way to access the property in December weather was by snowmobile. Christmas for the Tiede family meant solitude, opening presents by a warm fire, and quality family time with no distractions. None of them, in their wildest nightmares, could have imagined what fiendish horrors awaited them at their beloved family cabin that festive season.

As the Tiedes were doing some last-minute errands before heading back to the cabin, two parolees on the lam were busy making themselves at home in "Tiede's Tranquility." They ate the food in the fridge, opened the family's Christmas presents, and Edward Deli even used their phone to call a friend. The conversation quickly went from pleasantries to macabre: Deli told his friend he was readying to "shoot some people." Whether or not his friend thought he was joking, both Deli and his fellow criminal Von Taylor were deadly serious about their murderous intentions.

Deli then spotted something of interest: the family camcorder. He picked it up and filmed Taylor ripping through the gifts the Tiede family had bought one another. There are snippets online of this recording, although the full tape has never been released for public viewing. The parts I've viewed show Von Taylor, with unkempt hair, chewing his gum like an enthusiastic cow, ripping through the Christmas presents while doing a running commentary on them.

As the criminals were rifling through the Tiede's belongings, the family was heading back to the cabin. They were coming in separate vehicles, with Linae, Beth, and Kaye getting there first at about 3:30 pm. They had bags of shopping with them, but Linae told her mother and grandmother that she needed to run into the cabin quickly to warm her freezing hands under the hot tap. As she raced inside, she spotted one of her cousins in there, hiding behind the fridge, ready to jump out and scare her. However, when the figure leaped out in front of Linae, she was shocked to see it wasn't her cousin at all: it was a strange man aiming a pistol directly at her.

Kaye had followed her daughter into the cabin, and when she caught up with Linae, was horrified to see an unknown man pointing a gun at her child. Just as she was digesting the terror that had arrived at the once serene spot of peacefulness, another man appeared, pointing a gun directly at Kaye. The man wore thick glasses, had a mop of disheveled hair, and had a terrifying look on his face. Edward Deli walked towards Kaye as she pleaded to know why they were there. "I'll give you whatever you want," she reasoned with the intruders. The men stayed silent. Kaye began to pray aloud but was warned not to by Taylor. They worshiped the devil, he told her: no amount of praying would save her. Then, an awful bang rang in the air, and Kaye fell to the floor, blood covering her face.

Beth had also entered the property at this point, unaware of the vile intruders and their wicked plans for the family. She, too, was shot in the head. Linae had just witnessed the murder of her mother and grandmother and knew her sister and dad were due to arrive at the cabin imminently. The young woman kept the killer duo talking, trying to buy some time to get the intruders out of the house before the rest of the family arrived. "There's a car in the garage," she offered the men, hoping they'd take the keys and take off. Linae then heard the sound of snowmobiles. Her dad and sister were here; she needed to make sure the killers didn't get a chance to get near them. She led the men down to the garage and tried her best to get them to take the vehicle. While doing so, the ripping sound of the snowmobiles got louder. Rolf and Trish were outside the cabin. Linae's heart dropped.

The intruders readied their guns, walked out of the garage, and ordered the man and his daughter into the cabin. Rolf could see his eldest daughter had already fallen victim to the two hostage-takers and looked at Linae as tears rolled down her face. He was yet to find out that his wife and mother-in-law had already been mercilessly and senselessly slaughtered by the intruders.

The criminals demanded Rolf give them any money he had, and the distraught dad-of-two emptied his pockets and threw the cash on the floor for the men. After doing so, Von Taylor instructed Deli to shoot

Rolf. Deli raised his gun, but it misfired. Taylor raised his gun, which also clicked but wouldn't shoot. The fumbling criminals couldn't get their guns to fire, and their hostages stood frozen, unsure of what to do. Again, Taylor pulled the trigger. The gun didn't fire. Frustrated, he pulled the trigger yet again. Rolf collapsed to the ground, the gunshot to his face rendering him incapacitated. Trish and Linae were devastated as they watched their father meet the same fate as their mother and grandmother. But they knew the ordeal wasn't over yet: they'd spotted some gas cans brought up from the garage and wondered what was next. Were they going to be set on fire? Were they going to be forced to set their family cabin alight?

The killers picked up the gas cans and doused the entire place, including Rolf. They set it alight and demanded the girls jump on the snowmobiles and drive them away. The two men sat on the back of a snowmobile each as Linae and Trish drove their attackers through the blizzard. The younger sibling even thought about crashing into a tree to throw her captor off and escape, but that was too risky: it would possibly mean having to leave Linae behind while she got help, something she wasn't willing to do.

As the girls were speeding through the snow, Randy Zorn, the girls' uncle, was making his way to the cabin. He saw his nieces on the snowmobiles with some men on the back who he'd never seen before. Assuming they were perhaps their boyfriends, Randy waved at the girls. The sisters ignored him. He knew they'd seen him and was baffled as to why they would blank him; it certainly wasn't like them.

Linae and Trish made sure not to acknowledge their uncle, knowing that if they did, he'd meet the same fate as the rest of their family. Eventually, they came to the car park where everyone would leave their cars to swap for a snowmobile to drive up the Utah mountains. Here, the girls handed their captors the keys to the family car, and Taylor and Deli threw their guns into the vehicle. Linae spotted Taylor's knife inside his jacket as he loaded the car up. He noticed she'd spotted it and warned her that he was as good with a knife as he was with a gun. It seems Taylor had forgotten the episode with the gun moments earlier, where both he and his partner in crime were fumbling and misfiring their weapons like a pair of bumbling cartoon villains. Perhaps it would be a blessing for the girls if Von Taylor *was* just as capable with a knife as he was with a gun.

After forcing the girls into the back of the car, they spotted a familiar face - it was Randy again. He waved as he did before but yet again found himself ignored by his nieces. As he stood, baffled by the girls blanking him, he spotted something even more baffling: a man on a snowmobile, just a t-shirt keeping him warm in the freezing weather, with his face various shades of crimson and one eye swollen shut. The bloody-faced man had what Randy would describe as "bloodsicles" hanging from his face. As he got closer, it turned out it was his brother, Rolf Tiede.

Rolf pulled up beside Randy, his eyesight so poor he didn't recognize that it was his brother. "My wife and mother-in-law have been killed, and my daughters have been kidnapped," he cried, exasperated and desperate. By some miracle, Rolf had survived the bullet to the face and the house fire. He was wearing next to nothing because he had to strip himself of the flaming clothes to stop from getting engulfed in the fire. He scrambled his way out of the burning house and jumped on a snowmobile in search of help. Randy, shocked but determined to save his brother and nieces, helped his brother into his car.

In 1990, cell phones were certainly not commonplace, much less having one equipped in your car. Luckily, Randy had one in his vehicle and called 911. The signal was iffy in the mountains, and every time he dialed, he wasn't able to connect. He kept trying, though, and luckily, one of the calls went through to an operator. As he was on the phone with the police, he caught up with the Tiede family Lincoln, where the girls were locked in the back. This meant he could give authorities the exact location of the culprits as he kept on their tail. A 90-mile-per-hour chase took place, with Taylor and Deli doing their best to make off scot-free with their two hostages. One can only assume why the pair kept the girls alive and what they intended to do with them should they have escaped, but thankfully, it never got to that point.

Summit County Sheriff's Department was hot on the tail of the speeding Lincoln, and in their haste to escape, the killers lost control of the vehicle, and the car flipped multiple times down an embankment. Yet again, another miracle appeared in a horrific situation. Linae and Trish crawled out from the wreckage unscathed, physically at least. They raised their arms in the air as police approached them, letting officers know they were the captives and their attackers were still in the vehicle. They approached the car, dragged the killers out, and laid them on the snowy ground as they cuffed them.

Meanwhile, Ralph was a few miles back at a gas station with Rolf. While on the phone to 911, he told the dispatcher he needed a helicopter for his brother, who was close to death. Frustratingly, the call dropped before the operator heard this request. With Rolf fading away before his eyes, Ralph pulled into a gas station to use a payphone. Here, he got back through to the operator, and a helicopter was dispatched. Once it arrived and set off with Rolf, Randy was left with the sinking feeling that this was the last time he'd ever see his brother. He also questioned if he'd ever get to see his two nieces again.

Von Lester Taylor and Edward Steven Deli were charged with murder, attempted first-degree kidnapping, and aggravated kidnapping. Other charges, such as arson, theft, and failing to stop when police signaled them to, were also brought against them. In their 1991 trial, the killer pair listened to brave Linae and Trish's testimonies, where they recounted the hellish events that occurred the previous year at their once-serene cabin. However, unbeknown to Taylor and Deli, there was another person to take the stand, and it would make their jaws visibly drop.

As Rolf Tiede walked through the courtroom and took the stand, his attackers wore a shocked yet deflated look. Yet another witness - one they'd thought they'd killed - had arrived to offer up even more damning evidence against them. The Tiede family hadn't been destroyed to the extent the killers had thought. The Tiedes would now come together as a family to support each other and reminisce about the loved ones they'd senselessly lost. The killers had nothing but a lifetime in jail and the possibility of the death sentence ahead of them.

In May 1991, Von Lester Taylor was handed the death penalty. Edward Deli was given life behind bars.

A decade later, Deli wrote a letter to Linae, expressing sorrow over his actions and explaining how he was no longer the same person who committed the atrocious acts in the Utah mountains in 1990. It took her years, but she eventually decided to lift the burden from herself and forgive Deli. Still, forgiving isn't forgetting, and the sisters maintain that Deli should remain behind bars for the murders of their mother and grandmother. After all, forgiveness isn't always given because the offender deserves it, but rather because the victim deserves peace.

Taylor, on the other hand, wasn't as remorseful for his actions. He launched various appeals against his death sentence, something that's sure to reopen old wounds for the Tiede family. Taylor argues that Beth and Kaye were killed by Deli's gun, not his gun, and that Deli is the true murderer. He also insists that he was shocked when his companion killed the two victims. The courts agreed with this, and in 2020, Von Taylor had his death sentence overturned.

However, this decision was reversed in 2021, and Taylor was once again sentenced to die by lethal injection.

Linae and Trish went on to have families of their own, not letting the undeniably traumatic events of December 1990 spell out the rest of their lives. Rolf, the girls' hero, sadly passed away in 2008 after a battle with cancer. The cabin, having been burnt to the ground by Deli and Taylor, was rebuilt by the family, where they remade "Tiede's Tranquility" for generation after generation to enjoy and pay their respects to the family members who needlessly lost their lives there.

# The Tucson Pied Piper

This tale of terror began back in 1942 in Tucson. Charles and Katharine Schmid, affluent owners of a nursing home in Arizona, adopted a baby boy a day after he was born to parents out of wedlock. They named him Charles, after his adoptive father, although as the boy grew, he would find himself clashing with his dad. Still, despite the animosity between father and son, Charles was undeniably spoiled. Whatever he asked for, he got, rarely having to work too hard for it.

While he was far from academic, he did well socially in school. His athleticism, charisma, and good looks made high school a breeze for young Charles, although this didn't stop him from telling outlandish lies and feeling the need to be a braggart among his peers. There was undeniable insecurity for Charles; he would crush beer cans and place them in his boots to make him appear taller than he was. This caused him to walk with a slight limp. If someone questioned him as to why he walked the way he did, he would tell a story about how he sustained a leg injury while fighting members of the mafia.

It also seemed the youngster couldn't help himself from carrying out random acts of petty criminality. Just before graduation, Charles was caught red-handed stealing tools from the school. Why he did this is anyone's guess since he wanted for nothing, particularly since he likely had tools at the family home if he needed them. He also wasn't short of money - his parents gave him a healthy allowance of a few hundred dollars a month, and he had his own quarters at his parents' house. That few hundred bucks Charles was given each month works out at a few thousand dollars today - not bad for a teenager. He was also gifted a car and a motorcycle, other luxuries that the entitled young man didn't have to work for.

After leaving school, he began altering his appearance. He dyed his hair a striking black, wore make-up (notably, he drew a mole on his face to make him look "meaner"), and even tried stretching his bottom lip to make it look like Elvis'. Although we may now look back at his appearance and think it bizarre, Charles didn't lack female attention. Alongside his friends John, Richie, and Paul, he would cruise Speedway Boulevard in Tucson, and together, they'd pick up girls and drink alcohol. It seemed Charles Schmid had acquired something of a cult following among the girls in the area, although they were often younger than him and could be described as easily controlled by him.

It seemed nothing Charles did could satisfy his boredom or lust for power and dominance. While drinking with his friend John Saunders and girlfriend Mary French, Charles told the pair, "I want to kill someone tonight; I think I can get away with it." His impressionable friends didn't scold Charles for his sick comments, but instead, they agreed to help him carry out his vile desires.

First, they needed a victim. The group crawled the streets looking for the perfect girl, which just so happened to be 15-year-old Alleen Rowe. The trio drove up to her, wound the window down, and struck up a conversation with the girl. She was convinced to go on a double date with Mary, John, and Charles. Perhaps the fact there was another girl in the group put Mary at ease, and she hopped in the car, but the "date" never materialized. The gang drove Alleen to the desert where she was horrifically raped by Charles. He then told John to do the same to the hysterical girl, but he couldn't.

Mary sat in the car as the two men carried out their sick attack on Alleen. She turned the radio up to avoid hearing the screams, which ended when Charles picked up a big rock and smashed it into the teenager's skull multiple times. After the murder, all three members helped bury the girl's body in a shallow grave in the desert.

Ever the braggart and attention-seeker, Charles couldn't keep his wrongdoing to himself. He told his friend Richie Burns about the rape and murder, boasting about his callous acts without remorse. It became something of an open secret among the Tucson teens that Charles was a killer, but they were too afraid to go to the police. Moreover, many of the teens looked up to Charles, meaning they didn't want their idol to be locked up for his crimes.

When she didn't come home, Alleen's mother reported her daughter missing. The police assumed the girl was a runaway and didn't look too deeply into her sudden disappearance.

As well as dating Mary, Charles was seeing a number of other women, one of whom he confided in about Alleen's murder. Gretchen Fritz, like Charles, was born into affluence. Gretchen's father was a heart surgeon and an important community leader in Tucson, and the 17-year-old lived a comfortable lifestyle with her younger sister, Wendy. When Charles told her of his murderous past, she didn't go to the police or end the relationship. Their partnership would eventually come to an acrimonious end, however, and Gretchen would threaten to go to the authorities about Charles' confession.

After a short while stewing over Gretchen's threat, Charles decided she was too much of a risk. On August 16, 1965, he coldly strangled the girl to death. He also strangled Gretchen's little sister, Wendy, to death. She was 13 years old. Charles then dumped the girls' bodies in the desert before taking off.

James Fritz, the girls' father, had about just as much luck with getting the police to investigate his daughter's disappearance as Alleen Rowe's mother did. Despite the family being prominent members of the community, police were hesitant to label Gretchen and Wendy as anything other than runaways. After all, Gretchen was a "psychopath" and a "liar," according to her school teachers, and the police assumed the wayward teen had taken off with her sister and they would be back. The Fritzs knew something sinister had happened, and astonishingly, so did other people in the community.

You could bank on Charles to brag about his hideous crimes, and the attention-seeker unloaded his twisted secret to his friend, Richie Bruns. He went one step further than just recounting the murders - he even took Richie to the desert to look at the bodies before instructing his friend to help him bury the decomposing remains.

Richie, like the rest of Charles' cohort, didn't go to the police. Perhaps the shock of what he'd seen in the desert or the fear of repercussions stopped him in his tracks. But, as time passed, something entered Richie's life that changed his mind about going to the police about his dangerous friend. Darlene Kirk had an on-off relationship with Charles, but Richie had begun to take a liking to her, which was the catalyst in shifting the teenager from another of Charles' loyal minions to the person who would finally speak up.

Richie had convinced himself that Darlene was going to be next on Charles' hit list and took to hanging out with her at her house to make sure the girl was safe. This led to Darlene's parents thinking the young man was bothering their daughter, and eventually, they called the police on him for harassment. When authorities caught up with Richie, they advised him to get out of town, which he did. He spent three months in Ohio with his grandparents, but he couldn't shake the feeling that Darlene was in grave danger. His hunch could have been correct, but thankfully, we'll never know: Richie, overwhelmed with guilt over the Fritz murders and concerned about his crush's wellbeing, confessed to his grandmother about Charles Schmid. Now that the truth was out, Richie was convinced to tell the authorities what he knew, and he got in touch with the Tucson police department.

While all this was going on, Charles' behavior was reportedly becoming increasingly erratic and uncontrollable. He was still dating multiple girls, mostly underage, and while Richie had been spending his time in Ohio mustering up the courage to turn Charles in, the killer had married a 15-year-old girl after a blind date. By early November 1965, police caught up with Schmid, and the shocking tale gripped the Tucson locals, with the story making headline news for The Arizona Daily Star multiple times. The press dubbed Charles Schmid the "Pied Piper of Tucson" and reported on how he engaged in underage sexual activities with young girls from the area, how he exposed them to alcohol and drugs, and used the story to question the dark path Tucson youth seemed to be going down.

There was also the big question that no one could seem to answer: *why*? These girls all suffered a horrific end at the hands of a seemingly intelligent and charismatic young man with the world at his feet. Why did he feel the need to snuff out the lives of these young girls? Richie would offer up an answer for his former friend: boredom. Charles was a rich kid, he wanted for nothing, and had no boundaries or rules laid out by his parents. So, to seek out thrills, he went to extreme lengths. The sleepy city of Tucson offered little for its youth, said Richie, and there was nothing to do but cruise Speedway Boulevard, make out, or find mischief. Sadly, Charles' version of mischief took three young girls from their families forever.

Charles Schmid's trial began in 1966, and he insisted he killed no one, but he did know who the murderer was: Richie Bruns. The jury saw through his blame-shifting and sentenced him to death. As the gas chamber awaited him, Charles tried bargaining with the police. He finally agreed to show police where he buried Alleen Rowe because he insisted this would prove his innocence. The jury was told he'd bashed her head in, and this simply wasn't true, he persisted.

Once authorities saw Alleen's corpse, they'd see her skull was perfectly preserved, and then they'd be sure they'd sentenced an innocent man to death. Well, that's how Charles insisted events would pan out.

Charles, the police, and a news crew all headed to the desert where Alleen's crude grave was. Authorities watched as Schmid dug up the body. Perhaps some of them even believed that this would show that they'd gotten it wrong and that Schmid *was* the upstanding citizen he claimed to be - he was *that* believable. After a little while digging, Alleen's heavily broken skull could be seen clearly.

Charles' fight to avoid the chamber didn't last too long. The sentence was overturned when Arizona temporarily abolished the death penalty in 1971, and Schmid was handed 50 years behind bars instead. This allowed the killer to be housed with other prisoners, where he explored his newfound love of poetry in writing workshops, becoming one of the class's star writers. His poetry era didn't mesh well with his serial killer persona, so he changed his name to Paul David Ashley to reflect his new character. His prison teacher noted that he felt like Schmid learned to care about other people during this period.

However, as an outsider, it's perhaps easy to come to the conclusion that Charles' charisma and likability had swayed the lecturer's opinion of the killer. He could have been, of course, correct in his assessment, but his actions during a successful prison escape suggest otherwise to me.

In late 1972, Schmid and a fellow convicted murderer managed to flee the prison by climbing over the fence. The pair had planned this for a while, taking the time to earn each other's trust before finally taking their chance and jumping the wall in the bitter November weather. The duo entered a ranch and took the four occupants hostage for a short while before heading their own ways. Charles Schmid had been all over the newspapers a few years prior, so it was no surprise that he was recognized by a railroad worker. Despite donning a possibly comical blonde wig in order to hide his true identity, Schmid was spotted and arrested two and a half days after his escape. His fellow escapee was also apprehended, and the pair were back behind bars without tasting much freedom at all.

Poetic justice is often a phrase used when a killer is murdered, along with the use of the word "karma". In this case, with Schmid's newfound love of poetry, I'll use poetic justice to sum up what certain people may have felt about Charles Schmid's death.

On March 20, 1975, he was violently attacked by two prisoners armed with shanks. The pair slashed and stabbed, causing 47 separate stab wounds. Some of those were to his face. One of his eyes had been ripped out and his insides had been skewered by the homemade weapon. He was found by a prison guard, who noted the killer was covered head to toe in his own blood. Charles Schmid died ten days later. He was buried in the prison cemetery.

# Like A Woman Scorned

True crime has long been known to be emotionally provocative, and for good reason too. We read stories about people just like us being attacked, children just like the ones we love being abused, and certain groups or minorities being targeted. We are naturally drawn into these tales because they resemble horrors that could impact our own lives.

With that being said, true crime is often accused of sensationalizing such tales in order to sell more news subscriptions or gain more viewers for TV shows. Shocking words like "cannibalism," "decapitation," "dismembered," and "sexual assault" all tend to pique people's interest, even those who don't have a deep interest in crime. While these true crime buzzwords certainly attract attention, it's rare they all appear in the same headline. The case of Omaima Nelson, however, lived up to its horrific headlines. While the headlines may have looked like a classic case of true crime cliche clickbait, sadly, they weren't.

Omaima Nelson had the world at her feet. She was an attractive 23-year-old model who nannied alongside other side jobs to supplement her income. She had the "look" that was sought after for models of the '80s: olive skin, dark hair, catlike eyes, and a slim figure. When she met Bill Nelson, it seemed like the life she'd dreamed of for so long was about to become a reality. However, what ensued was nothing short of nightmarish.

Omaima was born in Egypt in the late sixties but moved to America as a teenager to take her slice of the American Dream. After all, she had nothing to lose: her life in Egypt was nothing short of hellish.

When she was young, she was subjected to the controversial (and, thankfully, now-banned) practice of female genital mutilation, often called "FGM" or "female circumcision". This traumatic event understandably stayed with Omaima, but it wouldn't be her last disturbing experience during childhood. Omaima told how her father was brutally abusive towards her and her mother, both sexually and physically, and the pair found themselves under the relentless control of the sadistic man. When her mother finally found herself able to leave her cruel and domineering husband, she took her daughter to Cairo. Despite living in Egypt's bustling and metropolitan capital, the family found themselves still living on the breadline. They resided in a slum known as "City of The Dead", where their modest shack was sandwiched among tombs.

Omaima's luck seemed to change, however, when she met an oil worker from America. After a brief stint dating, the pair got married. While the marriage didn't last, it did get Omaima over to the States to start a new life, albeit not with the man she'd just wed. She was still learning English, so job opportunities weren't plentiful, and the woman found herself floating from relationship to relationship to help her get by. She managed to get a few jobs nannying here and there, and modeling gigs offered a little cash, but they weren't regular enough to sustain her. Her main bread and butter, it seemed, was men.

She would meet a new suitor and move in with him incredibly quickly, using his money and resources at her leisure. She would often end the relationship abruptly by taking off without so much as a farewell, not before robbing the poor man of money and possessions, however. One of her boyfriends did manage to get a face-to-face break-up from her: she tied him up and threatened him with a gun before robbing him.

Initially settling in Texas, Omaima's lifestyle took her all over the U.S., swindling and robbing to get by. She eventually settled in the warm climate of Orange County, California, where she would meet her next husband, 56-year-old Bill Nelson.

Bill was well-to-do, owning fancy cars, lots of land, and boasted ownership of impressive properties. The cowboy boot-wearing man was a generous, larger-than-life character who was known to flash his wads of money around, something that perhaps attracted Omaima towards him when they met in a bar in the autumn of 1991. Bill's attraction to the younger woman was immediate, and after a few games of pool and pitchers of beer, the pair became inseparable. They quickly got married, although Bill didn't tell his new wife that he had a big secret: he was already married to someone else legally.

Still, after the wedding, the pair took off on their honeymoon to Bill's native Texas before returning to their Costa Mesa home. Despite the age gap, to the outside, the couple seemed to be settling into married life well. While Bill's children were initially apprehensive about his new wife and her possible ulterior motives for marrying their dad, they were coming round to the idea.

By Thanksgiving 1991, though, the honeymoon phase was well and truly over.

On that fateful holiday evening, Omaima stood next to the stove with the pans bubbling over, throwing waste into the garbage disposal. Instead of delicious food boiling away, it was her husband's body parts. Instead of throwing away unwanted food, it was Bill's remains. The young woman had brutally killed him before chopping him up and cooking his head and hands. Using an iron, she beat her husband to death, then dismembered him, even going as far as castrating him.

Omaima spent the next few days disposing of her 6' 4", 230-pound husband. It was proving tricky, so she decided to enlist the help of a former boyfriend, Jose Esquivel. She hopped in Bill's red sports car and headed to Jose's in the early hours of December 1. Omaima banged as loudly as possible on his door, but since Jose didn't recognize the fancy car parked up outside his home, he chose to ignore the early morning caller. Eventually, Omaima gave up but returned later that afternoon. Curious as to who the mystery visitor in the flash car was, Jose answered the door. He was surprised to see it was a woman he'd dated the year previously, and she had a big favor to ask him: to help him dispose of her dead husband.

Omaima was sporting cuts and bruises, which tied in with the story she gave Jose; that her violent husband, who frequently raped and beat her, had taken it too far on Thanksgiving. In a fit of rageful self-defense, she hit him over the head, unintentionally killing him. Omaima offered Jose a large sum of money to help her get rid of the body, and Jose agreed and told her to head back to her apartment while he arranged the body disposal.

As soon as Omaima drove off, Jose ran to the phone and, in a panic, called the police.

Authorities traced Bill's Corvette and found Omaima in the driver's seat. Bill - or rather, pieces of him - sat next to her in the passenger seat. Despite the officers finding remains next to her, the killer insisted that her husband was away on a business trip. To explain away the human parts she was found with, she blamed that on Bill, telling officers that he'd killed someone. Understandably, police weren't buying what the woman was telling them, no matter how much she insisted that Bill was alive and well. Authorities obtained a warrant to search the Nelson residence, and what they found would be worse than anybody could imagine.

Bags were filled with organs and body parts. The once-white marital bed sheets were covered in bright red blood, and the frame was broken, most notably the posts. The bathroom was a particularly gruesome scene: a torso hung up over the bathtub, which was full of blood and flesh. An iron was found, with hair and tissue stuck to it. In the kitchen, instead of a Thanksgiving dinner, the used pots and pans contained human parts. Most macabrely, the deep-fat fryer had cooked human hands inside it.

The fridge was the next place the police dared to look. Although they likely knew what to expect by this point, discovering a frozen human head is still bound to be a shock to happen upon. A closer look at the head revealed it was charred, leading police to believe it had been deep-fried before being preserved in the freezer.

It was clear to see that Omaima was bang to rights. Clear to everyone but Omaima, that is. She chopped and changed her story the more she was interviewed, sometimes even suggesting a demon-like voice had driven her to chop Bill up and cook his remains. Other times, she'd insist Bill was still alive. Then, she'd switch up her story and confess to killing Bill, but was forced to do so since she was a victim of his abuse, both physical and sexual. She did have injuries on her face and body that could suggest she'd been attacked, but these injuries could also have been self-sustained while dismembering a human.

While Omaima was being interviewed by police, the medical examiner was tasked with trying to find out the truth by analyzing Bill's remains; the ones that were found, anyhow. There were still over 100 pounds of Bill that hadn't been uncovered, but the examiner did the best they could with what they had. It was enough to confirm that Bill had been castrated and disemboweled, two incredibly rage-fueled acts of violence that were carried out after the murder. His skull was fractured, which tied in with the blood-spattered iron found at the murder scene. On Bill's ankles were ligature marks, suggesting the man was tied up at some point, either before or after death.

The likelihood of ever finding the rest of Bill was getting bleaker by the minute. Neighbors had heard the Nelson's garbage disposal buzzing away for hours that Thanksgiving but didn't assume it was anything sinister. It looked like the missing parts of the victim had been truly disposed of by Omaima.

The suspect wasn't relenting in her outlandish claims to police, either. Her confessions and subsequent recanting of these admissions caused police to become weary of Omaima, but they must have been shocked by her claims that she cooked her husband to eat him. In fact, she gave startling details of how she cooked and ate his ribs in BBQ sauce and noted how "sweet" the meat she consumed was. Like her other admissions of guilt, this was later denied by Omaima. While authorities weren't sure what was true or what was fabricated, they were sure of one thing: Omaima was a murderer. In December 1992, the trial took place.

The defense told the court about Omaima's difficult childhood, filled with sexual abuse, beatings, and poverty. Despite Bill and Omaima only being wed for a month, the court heard how he would abuse her, raping her and assaulting her on a regular basis. The lead-up to Bill's death was the breaking point for his wife and also the worst the abuse had ever been, Omaima would say. She had been tied up on the marital bed, unable to escape for days, while Bill repeatedly violated her. It was only when she managed to wriggle herself free that she bludgeoned him to death, then took a pair of scissors to his lifeless body and began stabbing him. It was at this point the suspect lost her memory and had no recollection of cutting Bill up or disposing of him. The psychologist Omaima had been sent to while awaiting trial diagnosed her with PTSD as well as expressing signs of psychosis.

This would explain Omaima telling the police that her ancient ancestors spoke to her and told her to kill her husband and scatter his remains.

While the story about the restraints had some believability due to the bed knobs on the blood-stained bed being broken, the prosecution brought forward their own damning evidence.

They had managed to piece together that fateful Thanksgiving evening, telling the courtroom how Bill had been tied up as part of a consensual intimate session, his feet and wrists bound to the bedposts. As Omaima had done in the past, the prosecution suggested that once Bill was tied up, she demanded money from him. Either Bill broke free, explaining the broken posts, or struggled enough to damage the bed. Regardless of how this part of the story went, the next part is irrefutable: Omaima beat Bill over the head, then used the scissors to mutilate him. Then, she dismembered him and cooked various body parts.

The trial came to a head in January 1993, where Omaima was acquitted of the first-degree murder, but was found guilty of second-degree murder, resulting in life behind bars, with a minimum of 28 years. She was sent to the Central California Women's Facility to serve her time.

Prison can be a good way for criminals to reflect on their wrongdoings, to find remorse for their crimes, and to seek to better themselves as human beings. It seems Omaima's hustle remained while she was in jail, as she began a relationship with a disabled elderly man, with the gentleman in question visiting California for conjugal visits. The pair soon married. Since the man was frail and unwell, it wasn't long before Omaima was yet again a widow, but this time, she acquired a lot of money from her late spouse.

What good is money when you're in jail, though? Perhaps it can buy creature comforts or friends in the right places, but no doubt it will help Omaima when she's eventually freed. She applied for parole in 2006 but was still considered too dangerous to be let out. Her coldness toward the crimes she'd committed was plain to see. It was noted she refuses to accept accountability for the murder, much less show repentance for it, which is why she was again refused parole in 2011. The next time she'll be eligible to apply for release is 2026, although it seems unlikely (as of writing this) that she'll show the remorsefulness and penitence needed to prove to the parole board that she's changed.

# A Most Sadistic Gang

Even for the most hardened true crime follower, there will come a time when you find a case that just punches you in the gut. For me, the story of Junko Furuta caused me to spend weeks researching the case, even going as far as getting the court documents translated from Japanese to English to gain a better understanding of the especially disturbing case. While this chapter isn't about the Junko case - I'm considering covering her case in greater depth in a future publication - the tale of Jennifer Ertman and Elizabeth Pena gave me the same crushing blow when I learned about it.

Jennifer Ertman and Elizabeth Pena's lives had barely begun before they were cruelly snuffed out by a gang of boys not much older than they were. Still, the vile acts carried out by the group of violent teens were far from child's play, and their lack of empathy during and after their despicable rape and murder of the two girls defies belief.

Jennifer and Elizabeth met at Waltrip High School in Houston, Texas in 1992. Jennifer was a mild-mannered girl who rarely found herself in any kind of trouble. The 14-year-old had just recently begun experimenting with wearing make-up, and although described as a modest youngster, she had a fun sense of humor and was known to be warm and kind-hearted.

Jennifer befriended Elizabeth when the 16-year-old transferred to Waltrip after a spate of rebelliousness. Elizabeth, like most teens tend to, had been acting out, and her parents hoped the move to a new school would help their wayward daughter get on the straight and narrow. When she met Jennifer, it seemed like this would be Elizabeth's turning point; the younger girl proved to be a source of positive influence, and both sets of parents approved of the friendship.

The pair would often visit one another's house, hanging out after and during school, and their bond grew quickly throughout the spring and summer of 1993. There were other members of the friendship group, too, one of whom was Gina Escamilla. The teen lived in Spring Hill Apartments, which had a pool. Perfect for summer nights, the three girls made the most of the amenity, with Gina often having friends over in the warm evenings as they gossiped and talked about school. Elizabeth had an 11:30 pm curfew, which Jennifer was always sure to remind her friend of to ensure she didn't get into trouble.

On June 24, 1993, the trio of girls had arranged to meet for a pool party at Spring Hill. Jennifer was dropped off at Elizabeth's house that afternoon, then the pair were given a lift to Gina's house later that day by Elizabeth's mother. Melissa Pena was sure to remind her daughter about the agreed curfew, to which her daughter reiterated that she would be home on time. Plus, she had Jennifer with her, who was a reliable young girl and helped make sure her friend kept out of trouble. Because of this, Melissa wasn't too worried about her daughter missing curfew but liked to remind her it was in place for a reason. The teens excitedly jumped out of the car, looking forward to the party and enjoying the sun.

Meanwhile, in a close-by suburb called White Oak, a group of thugs were readying themselves for a gang initiation. The initiation was violent, but Raul Villarreal was desperate to join the so-called "Black and White Gang", led by Peter Cantu. They named themselves this due to the mix of ethnicities within the group. Cantu was a known thug, with the 18-year-old already being on the police's radar for several violent offenses, but his sadistic streak didn't stop him recruiting a number of fellow teens into his gang.

In order to be welcomed into the group, Raul Villarreal had to fight other members of the gang until he was beaten. These were Derrick O'Brien, aged 18; Jose Medellin, aged 18; Efrain Perez, aged 17; and another teen named Roman Sandoval. Also in attendance were Frank Sandoval and Venancio Medellin, 14, relatives of some of the older gang members.

Villarreal had to last five to ten minutes fighting each member, and by the end of his third fight, he fell to the floor, unconscious. Bloodied and beaten, the teenager's fate was being discussed by the gang members; should they let him join based on his fighting performance? As they came to their unanimous conclusion, Villarreal awoke from his fuzzy slumber to Cantu congratulating him on being a newfound member of The Black and White Gang.

"You're a badass!" Cantu exclaimed while helping Villarreal to his feet, no doubt ecstatic that he was now part of the violent group he so longed to be part of. Despite his busted-up face and being covered in his own blood, the new gang member sat down with the peers who'd just pummeled him and drank beer, roughhoused, and planned the rest of their evening. It was decided they should continue their night near the railroad tracks.

Back at Spring Hill, the trio of girls laughed and joked the night away by the pool, and before they knew it, 11:30 was fast approaching. Of course, it was Jennifer, the sensible one, who noticed this and reminded Elizabeth that she'd be in trouble if she wasn't back on time. Not wanting to disappoint her parents, Elizabeth heeded her friend, and the pair headed home. To be extra sure they'd get back before the curfew, the girls thought they'd take a shortcut back to Elizabeth's house, a decision that would lead them to unimaginable horrors.

It's a frustrating thought that if the girls had walked home another way - a safer, albeit longer way - they'd quite probably be grown women now, possibly with children of their own. Their desire to stay out of trouble got them into the worst kind of trouble. The girls' shortcut took them to the same train tracks where The Black and White gang were drinking.

The two girls had picked up a brisk pace, not just because they were running late but because the rowdy gang began catcalling them. Jose Medellin initiated the unwanted groping of the girls, grabbing at Elizabeth, who batted his hands away from her. In retaliation, Jose followed the girls and taunted them, asking where they were going until he grabbed Elizabeth by the neck and forced her to the ground. He then pulled her along the harsh gravel-filled ground back to the rest of the gang. She cried, screamed, and pleaded with her attacker to let her go, to no avail. He also didn't heed her pleas for him to stop when he demanded she remove her underwear, which she was forced to do.

For Jennifer, it was fight or flight. We never know how we'd react in a situation like this until we're in it, and the right choice often isn't always the path our heart leads us down. Jennifer chose to fight that night, and despite Elizabeth's house being just a mile away, she ran toward the gang to protect her friend.

The gang easily overpowered the girl, and she found herself on the gravel, just like Elizabeth. At this point, Roman and Frank Sandoval told Cantu they were leaving since they didn't attack girls and weren't going to stick around to watch. Every other gang member repeatedly raped the girls.

For over an hour, the rabid gang of teen boys took turns to carry out their fiendish desires. No less than four times did each boy rape the girls. No amount of remorse, guilt, or empathy found its way to any of the attackers that night, even when Jennifer and Elizabeth struggled and pleaded with their rapists. The youngest there, Venancio Medellin, largely stood by and watched as the elder members assaulted the girls and reveled in their tears and fighting back. That was until Peter Cantu shouted over to the 14-year-old to join them and "get some." The boy obliged and joined in.

Heartbreakingly, during the assaults, the girls looked over at one another while being violated, helplessly offering the other the compassion and concern that eluded their attackers. Their weeping was of no concern to the boys, who, once they'd decided they'd had enough, spoke about their next steps. They could let the girls go, but they'd seen every one of their rapist's faces. Peter Cantu decided there was no other choice but to kill their victims. The gang didn't dispute this decision, either; "Get on your knees, bitch," new member Raul Villarreal yelled at the girls as soon as Cantu told him they had to die.

He ordered the group to take the girls to the woods to kill them but told Venancio to stay where he was because he was too young to watch what they were about to do. If you go by Cantu's logic, Venancio wasn't too young to carry out or watch a violent sex attack, though. Derrick O'Brien took off his nylon belt, and he and Jose Medellin wrapped it around Jennifer's neck and pulled on an end each. They pulled with such force that the belt broke.

They pulled Jennifer's shoelaces from her sneakers and pulled them tightly round her neck. This eventually killed her. The fear and panic she must have felt not just in her final moments is unimaginable, knowing almost for certain that this was her last minutes on Earth. To know she'd never see her mother and father again, that she'd never grow up, and that she'd never know the comfort of being at home again must have been overwhelmingly painful.

For Elizabeth, who had to endure watching the slow and excruciating murder of her best friend, the despair of her final moments was met with a burst of hope: she saw a window of opportunity and hopped up from the ground and fled. With the shoelace still wrapped around her neck, she raced away from the rabid pack of boys. Her race to freedom was cut dead with a brutal fist from Cantu to the head.

In retaliation for her trying to escape, the sadistic gang leader beat Elizabeth as she lay on the floor. With his steel-toe boots, he kicked her in the face multiple times, enough to cause the girl to lose a number of teeth. He also took his anger out on Jennifer, breaking her ribs in the process. The gang then strangled Elizabeth to death. To ensure there was zero chance of either girl miraculously surviving, the gang then began jumping on the victim's necks, taking turns to bounce on the lifeless bodies. Perhaps this was just to add insult to injury since the girls were already clearly dead by this point.

To add to their rap sheet that night, the group then stole anything of value from the girls. Jennifer, who was just beginning to experiment with jewelry, particularly necklaces, was wearing some of her favorite items the night she was killed. The little cash the girls had was also taken. Jennifer also had a cartoon watch that Cantu stripped her of, but would throw over to Venancio Medellin, stating he didn't want it.

After their pillage, the group headed back to Cantu's residence, where he lived with his brother Joe. When the gang entered the property, Christina Cantu, Joe's wife, noticed the group were all bloodied and disheveled. Medellin, despite being just 14, had a sinister reply to the woman's legitimate concern: he told her they'd been "having fun", and that their acts that night would likely be on the news. Unable to keep his mouth from running further, he blurted out that he'd raped two girls that night.

Peter Cantu didn't disagree with his young protégé's version of events and even pulled out the stash of jewelry that belonged to the girls. The group then shared out the loot. Jose Medellin made sure he got Jennifer's ring engraved with 'E' for his girlfriend. He was also overheard telling the rest of the crew how a gun would have been handy to have that night.

While Christina Cantu stayed quiet while she bore witness to the unsettling actions of her brother-in-law and his gang, as soon as they left, she went to Joe with her concerns. It was his little brother, though, and he struggled with the idea of handing him over to authorities. But, he ought to have had more empathy since his wife had been the victim of a gang rape herself, aged just 15.

Meanwhile, Jennifer and Elizabeth's families were in a state of panic. They'd not come home, and there had been no contact from them to say when they'd be back. Plus, Jennifer was super sensible, and Elizabeth wouldn't want to miss her curfew by a minute, let alone by hours. They knew something was amiss, but they would have no way of knowing the true horrors their daughters had endured just hours earlier.

The hours that passed with no contact from the girls turned into days. Flyers were put up, the police had been notified, and the community was anxious that the girls be found safe and sound. Four long days passed before the decomposing bodies of two teenage girls were found in T.C. Jester Park in White Oak. The police didn't happen upon the girls randomly, either. They'd received an anonymous phone call telling them where the teens were. Sure enough, just like the caller said, the bodies were found at the bayou.

With the tragic truth finally out, the police were tasked with finding the culprits. It wouldn't take them long; they simply traced the anonymous caller number, which led them to Joe Cantu's home. It had taken Christina four days, but she eventually got her husband to do the right thing. When police arrived at his residence, he gave them the names of all the culprits. The gang was swiftly arrested.

The evidence was irrefutable. The confessions spilled easily from each of the boys. From rabid boys to blubbering babies, a tough interrogation, it was not. They all admitted the part they played in the rapes and murders, as well as the part their fellow gang members played. Peter Anthony Cantu, the ringleader, was handed a death sentence. Jose Ernesto Medellin was also sentenced to death, as were Derrick Sean O'Brien, Efrain Perez, and gang newcomer Raul Omar Villarreal. Venancio Medellin, due to being 14 when he carried out the crime, was given 40 years behind bars.

However, the Supreme Court would eventually disallow the death sentence for those who committed their crimes under 18, which meant Medellin and Perez were spared from the lethal injection. Instead, they got life in jail. Both will become eligible for release in 2029. By 2029, Jennifer and Elizabeth would have been in their early 50s.

First to face their punishment in 2006 was Derrick O'Brien. He was followed by Jose Medellin in 2008. Both criminals would express their remorse over their 1993 actions, with anti-death penalty advocates using their repentance to argue against this form of punishment. Still, their apologies didn't wash with Elizabeth's father, who retaliated by saying he wished his daughter could have had as peaceful and painless a death as her killers. He remarked that Derrick O'Brien had passed away just twenty seconds after the needle hit his arm and that he wished instead that he endured what the girls did before his death.

Last to receive the death penalty was Peter Cantu. He was given the lethal injection in August 2010 after 17 years in jail.

Venancio Medellin has applied for parole multiple times, and each time, he has been rejected. He's up for release in 2034. He will be the same age Jennifer would have been should she have lived.

The girls' school, Waltrip, and the park they were found in both have memorials for them. They lie at Woodlawn Garden of Memories Cemetery.

# Mother Or Murderer?

As dawn was fast approaching in the peaceful area of Dalrock Heights, Texas, the birds were just beginning to stir. The sky was softening from the night darkness, and the residents of the affluent area were mostly still fast asleep. Most of them, but not all: one of them was awake and had particularly evil intentions.

June 6, 1996, was a memorable shift for Doris Trammell, one of the night dispatchers on duty at Rowlett Police Department. A panicked caller rang through in the early hours, barely coherent, but Doris managed to gather enough from the caller to understand the horrifying situation.

"Somebody broke into our house...they stabbed my babies!" the caller screamed, at which point Doris hurriedly dispatched medical assistance along with the police. She tried to calm the caller down, who was repeating that her children were dying in between horrified cries for help. Darlie Routier, a 26-year-old mother of three, was inconsolable, however - and who could blame her? Her five- and six-year-olds were laid in front of her, bloodied with eyes agape, on the brink of death.

Their names were Devon and Damon. The boys' dad, Darin, was upstairs when the attack happened and was awoken by his wife's screaming. He raced downstairs to see a most sickening sight - his eldest two boys lying in their own blood. Five-year-old Damon was on his front. Six-year-old Devon was on his back, the deep crimson lacerations on his tiny chest clear to see. As this father's world was collapsing around him in slow motion, he needed to think fast; the faint gurgles coming from Damon snapped Darin back to horrific reality, and he raced to unresponsive Devon to perform CPR. Damon was still breathing - for now. He would do his best to ensure both sons made it out alive.

Police arrived quickly, although the crime scene they tended to was not the norm for Rowlett PD. They had crime in the area, sure, but never something as evil and heinous as this. Officers advised Darlie to tend to Damon's bleeding wounds with a towel, a request she ignored. Instead of tending to her children, the hysterical woman was yelling at officers about the intruder who stabbed her and her children.

Concerned the attacker may still be lurking, officers traced the path of blood leading to the garage. Nothing there. They searched the rest of the house, hand on gun, just in case. No hiding place was left untouched by police, and although no culprit was found, they did make some interesting observations. A side window into the garage had been tampered with, and its screen had been slashed. A blood-stained knife lay nonchalantly on the kitchen worktop. Next to the weapon lay a money-filled purse and jewelry.

While police were trying to weigh up the situation, medics were trying to save the two young victims. The large knife wounds in their chests had reached their lungs. Devon, despite his father's best efforts, had suffocated to death. A truly horrifying way to go for anybody, let alone a child who could never have comprehended someone doing something so evil toward them. The six-year-old laid mere feet away from his younger brother, who, despite struggling for breath, was miraculously still alive. He was rushed to the ambulance with a team of medics ready to revive the child. He would sadly pass away before he got to the hospital.

Meanwhile, Darlie Routier was also being tended to by medics. She'd also felt the brunt of the attacker, albeit not as harshly as her boys. She had a knife wound on her neck, although not deep enough to cause any lasting damage. Darlie was unharmed enough physically to tell police her attacker was around six feet tall and wore all black.

Rowlett's law enforcement presence was ramped up at the Routier's property. Not only for protection but to gather any clues they may find. Suspicions began to arise over the true nature of the crime. At the very least, things weren't adding up. As soon as they could, the police wanted to know as much detail as they could from the only person who'd seen the murderer: Darlie. They also felt uneasy about a comment Darin made the night of the sickening attack: "I guess this is the biggest thing Rowlett's ever had," he casually said to an officer. Grief and shock can cause many strange behaviors, but this couldn't be ignored.

Other things piqued their uncertainty, too. Certain areas of the Routier home had been cleaned spotlessly the night of the murders after the murders. The sink, for example, had been wiped until it was shiny, but there were small spatters of blood all around it. This triggered a further look into other places in the house where blood may have been cleaned up. If you've ever watched Forensic Detectives, you'll know all about Luminol. It's a chemical that crime scene investigators use to make blood show up (and glow in the dark) even when it's been cleaned up. In this case, Luminol exposed that one of the boys' bloody handprints was wiped from the sofa.

A chat with Darlie found her story remained the same: an unknown man broke into the house via the window. However, the screen that had been slit for entry wasn't big enough for an intruder to climb through. On top of this, the bloody footprints that led to that window merely stopped dead at the window. No blood on the windowsill as the killer apparently climbed back out. No bloody handprints on the wall. It was like the killer walked to the window and simply stopped and evaporated. The crime scene, in general, looked odd. While there were some signs of a struggle, some items looked placed there, like it had been staged.

Nurses who tended to Darlie at Baylor Medical Center the night of the vicious killings also felt something wasn't adding up about the mother's reaction to seeing her baby boys in the trauma room. It was noted she looked over, saw her child covered in his own blood, and looked away. The response of no response set alarm bells ringing. There was no sobbing, no hysterics, no breakdowns.

Another police interview with Darlie proved to offer a few more details than the one prior. She explained how she awoke to a strange man on top of her that fateful night, and when she chased him through the house, he dropped his bloody knife and fled. Darlie picked it up and placed it on the counter. Something she shouldn't have done, she says, because now it only had her fingerprints on it, not the killers.

After being read her Miranda Rights, Darlie proceeded to offer a written statement to authorities. In this version, she explained how she recalled that young Damon was still walking about when she awoke to the strange man on her.

At the boys' funeral, a detective on the case overheard Darlie whispering she was sorry over their tiny caskets. He observed her throughout the heartbreaking day, noting that after apologizing to her babies, she began screaming about the killer. It was also noted that Darlie told funeral-goers that she wasn't worried about the cost of the funeral because she'd get $5,000 for it. Another disturbing observation was Darlie's lack of tears. Plenty of tissues were handed to mourning family members that day. Darlie was not one of them.

Again, grief affects you in strange ways. You will say and do things that are way out of the ordinary, and you'll look back and wonder what on earth you were thinking. Although, the next part of this tragic tale takes grief-induced actions to a new level if, indeed, they are grief-induced.

She held Devon's seventh birthday party at his graveside, inviting a handful of friends and family and a local TV crew to film it. It could perhaps have been considered a weird PR stunt if it weren't for Darlie being recorded spraying silly string over her deceased son's grave. Darlie nonchalantly chewed gum and joked with family while an overall weird posthumous birthday celebration was caught on camera.

Rowlett Police's suspicion of Darlie was now on red alert. There were way more questions than answers. The boys were killed senselessly. There was no robbery or motive for the crime. Darlie's purse was right where the intruder was alleged to have been. Why did the murderer run away from the woman who potentially could identify him? Why did he drop his weapon and not return for it, since it would have been damning evidence? In fact, why would he have used the Routier's knife instead of being equipped with his own? Thinking more about the weapon, since it belonged to the Routiers, it couldn't have been used to slash the window sheet. Why would such a brutal madman butcher two young boys but only leave superficial wounds on Darlie? It was clear: the attack on Damon and Devon was personal, fueled by emotion. Darlie's attack didn't reflect the same level of aggression.

Just days after the graveside spectacle, Darlie was arrested for the murder of her children.

The trial began in January 1997, with prosecutor Greg Davis opening the hearing by telling the jury how he would expose Darlie as a materialistic mother who would kill her own children for financial gain. The defense countered this suggestion by asking why would Darlie kill her sons for a few thousand dollars when she could have gotten closer to a million if she'd killed her husband?

The prosecution showed the damning silly string video. They noted the crime scene appeared staged. Defense countered by asking why Darlie would harm just two of her children yet leave one alive?

A chief medical examiner also took the stand in Darlie's defense, noting how the injury to her neck was incredibly close to her carotid artery and didn't look self-inflicted. His professional opinion differed greatly from those who treated Darlie on the night of the murders.

Prosecution had more evidence up their sleeve, though: the nightshirt Darlie wore that fateful day. They said the blood that spattered on the back of her nightwear got there when she lifted the butcher's knife over her head when stabbing her two boys.

The defense had a thought-provoking counter. Little Damon was still breathing when emergency services arrived, although a medical examiner had previously stated that the child lived for just eight minutes after the attack. Darlie's call with the police was logged for six minutes. This meant she would have had to stage the crime scene, inflict knife wounds on herself, and clean up the bloodied sink in less than two minutes.

Despite the defense team's best efforts, Darlie was found guilty of murder. She was handed the death penalty.

Not everybody was convinced that the guilty verdict was the right one. The community was torn. Sure, her actions after the event were deemed strange, but something about Darlie's sentence didn't sit well with some people who followed the case. A 2000 look back at the case on an episode of 20/20 brought some unknown facts to light.

The court transcript had tens of thousands of errors in it. A juror also admitted they hadn't seen the portion of the "silly string" video where it showed Darlie somber and grieving at the graveside of her boys. There was also a bloody fingerprint of an unknown adult found at the scene of the crime.

Another prominent supporter of Darlie is Barbara Davis, who previously wrote a book about Darlie's guilt. After this new evidence became public knowledge, she changed her opinion on the case and now donates any royalties from that book to Darlie's family.

The Routiers divorced in 2011.

It seems this case is far from open and shut. Some people are convinced of Darlie's guilt; others think the blame lies elsewhere, such as at Darin's feet. He had tried to enlist a criminal to burglarize his home as part of an insurance scam mere months before his boys were killed. Could it be that someone had tried to do just that, but for some warped reason, the children were harmed during a botched attempt?

There are still so many unexplained elements of this case that opinion is divided. What are your thoughts on this tragic case?

# Final Thoughts

Each one of the stories I've covered in this book is someone's reality. The victims and their families endured the horrors and the aftermath of the atrocities I've spoken about, and that fact is never lost on me. It's part of the reason this topic reels me in so much: the sense of injustice and frustration I feel when digesting true crime stories always somehow encourages me to learn more about each tale. Since you made it through to the end of this book, I'm guessing it's the same for you, too.

Thank you for picking this book up and taking the time to read it. Hopefully, I've made you aware of cases you'd not been aware of. That's my goal for this little *Macabre Yet Unknown True Crime Stories* series: to get those little-known crimes out there, to make sure the victims are never forgotten, and to remind people that awful crimes can happen to any of us. Stay vigilant out there, people, although, as a true crime reader, I already know you have a healthy dose of vigilance and gut instinct.

Once again, thank you so much for reading, and if you find the time to leave a review, that would be incredibly helpful to me and help get the book to a wider audience.

You can sign up to my newsletter here:

*Danielaairlie.carrd.co[1]*

---

1. *http://danielaairlie.carrd.co*

Printed in Great Britain
by Amazon

41192069R00062